Is the Coffee Fresh?

Is the Coffee Fresh?

drama...dysfunction...
and a magical dose of
divine intervention!

Marc Renson

Is the Coffee Fresh?
Drama...Dysfunction...and a Magical Dose of Divine Intervention!
Copyright © 2009 by Marc Renson

Cover design by Robert Barkowski
Interior layout by Melissa Mykal Batalin

Printed in the United States of America

The Troy Book Makers
www.thetroybookmakers.com

ISBN-13: 978-1-110158-759
ISBN-10: 1-440158-754

I dedicate this book to Greg Salomon.
Without you, Greg,
there would be no Ambition!
I wish you daisies.

photograph by Dylan Spencer

ACKNOWLEDGMENTS

Writing this book has been challenging for me on many levels and I'd be an absolute liar if I took all the credit. In life, I've found that for a person to be successful, one must surround oneself with success. My success here is my staff, all of whom have contributed something of themselves to make Ambition what it is. More success has come from other extraordinary people who have entered my life at the very moment they were needed most. My partner Greg Salomon, who saw and still sees the best in me, no matter how dysfunctional I am. Michael Sugarman allowed me five months of his life reading and rereading every sentence. Greg and Julie Turgeon, I couldn't have asked for better friends who always have my back in the midst of danger. George Leobowitz, who originally read and without judgment corrected my mess of a first draft while adding some of his wonderful wit. Michael and Traci Samuel, Oh those mangoes! And Traci, I know your mom is proud of us. Is there anything we've missed through the years? Billy Spillane thanks for your cleverness. Ali Fritz and Dan Pohlig, I am indebted to you for your support, friendship, and a well needed glass of wine. Your restaurant choices are superb. Sarah Spence-Staulters, thank you for your kindness and sharing your life with a desperate wanna-be writer. Skip Whitson of Sun Publishing, my gratitude goes to you for reading my first chapter, pointing out the good, the bad, and offering your recommendations. No other editor gave me a chance or the time of day. Michael Garrett, thank you for editing, critiquing, and supporting my work. John Dalton, you've edited my words into a culinary masterpiece. Thank you for entering my life at the eleventh hour and for getting it done. Bob Barkowski, you saw my vision for the cover and you've constructed a masterpiece that nobody understands, like, why are the feathers pink? Arjun Parthasarathy, thank you for your last minute editing, talent, and gentle humor. Jacqueline Kraus, I didn't know a bookkeeper's job was being an editor also. Thank you for knowing word. All the friends I've met along the way, Vince Manti and Nancy Nicholson my food experts and traveling companions. Rich Bogardus and Chari Jones you two rock! And Rich and Chari if you don't buy a book, I'll blackmail you with the penis pasta picture! Everyone at DOT. Fred, Wilson, Frank, Bob H, Bob & Bill, Mary Ann, Heidi, Mike, Ozzy aka Mr Cubano, and all the others. There are just too many to mention. All my cheerleaders at the Lottery building Jenny, Kathy, Mary Jo, & Ms Vicky. You ladies are my Charlie's Angels. John from the Lottery building, I want my winning ticket already! All the merchants on Jay Street, lets show Schenectady what we can do!

Anne Smith and Melissa Batalin of The Troy Book Makers, huge hugs to you ladies. I heard the song "East Bound and Down" and that's what you ladies did—something that couldn't be done, you found a solution.

Kudos to my spirit guides for placing everyone that I needed in front of me when I asked for them and being patient while I took my first steps in this whole project. Thank you Madonna, Cyndi Lauper, Barbara Eden, Donna Summer, and Dolly Parton—without you ladies I would have lived a totally different life.

This accomplishment is something I never thought I would be able to achieve. Success, I believe, has been my biggest fear. I was told by a wise young lady not to be afraid, but instead, use that courage to guide myself. So with the publication of this book, I'm releasing my inhibitions and letting go of my fears, hesitations and all those insecurities. I couldn't have done this without you. Thanks to my entire family—Jim, Denise, Karen, Tom, Jessica, Edward, Jaclyn and Heather for always being there. I haven't forgotten but saved the best for last. Thank you, Mom. You'll always be my greatest superhero. And God, thank you for this life.

FORWARD

The book you're about to read is true (for the most part) and the names have been changed to protect the innocent, *if there are any left.*

The stories especially those about let's say the more challenging customers are sometimes horrendous, frightening, unbelievable and undeniably unreal, but the best part is they're funny. One of my favorite factors of being the author is remembering the episodes and now looking back and reading the stories, the humor it brings me. *Living it at the time, not-so-funny.*

I would also like to acknowledge that these stories were accumulated over a nine year period and that of the tens of thousands of customers that we have served faithfully and have sang our praises for almost a decade deserve the most recognition. For without them there would be no Ambition and without Ambition well…where would I be?

So without further ado, take it away maestro.

Grand Opening?

Monday, April 10, 2000, 11:38 a.m., Schenectady, New York. Two news reporters from local TV station—Channel 6—park their van and walk down Jay Street. One is carrying a camera with a light attachment. The other is carrying a microphone and a small briefcase. These two men are on their way to cover the story of a new restaurant's grand opening in a former downtown landmark tavern. They're looking at the dilapidated facade of the law firm and the struggling retail storefronts, most having newspapers taped to the windows due to a high decline of failed businesses from the past. The city once flourished, once overflowed with GE employees, steel workers, and train manufacturers all crowding the downtown streets, patronizing the local merchants— all businesses were once thriving. But on this day, only local banks, City Hall, Proctor's Theater, a historic Beaux-Arts vaudevillian theater, the Post Office and small businesses are open. There are two pizza shops, a deli, Open Door Bookstore, Two Spruce Pottery, and two smoke shops, one named Orion. Few people are walking about, the birds are chirping, and the nearby train can be heard whistling in the background. Residents and workers are finding their way back to the work-week routine on this typical Monday. The temperature is 52° and sunny. There's a pedestrian brick walkway in the center of downtown called Jay Street. This is the city's little diamond in the rough.

The reporters enter this new business called Ambition, look around and wonder if they're even in the right place. It couldn't possibly be here, they think, so they flag down the cook (me), a young (and handsome) man in his late twenties, a buzz cut, and white chef's coat and black pants. The cook's name is Marc and he's one of the owners.

They ask, "Is this where the grand opening is?" As they look around the restaurant, there are only six people currently in the building. There are two women sitting in a booth, a single Hispanic woman at the bar and three other people: two men and a young lady sitting at a table towards the back.

"Yes," replies Marc, "but the grand opening isn't starting until noon."

The news men look at each other with hesitation and start setting up their equipment. The man with the microphone checks himself in a mirror at the bar, matting his hair down with his hand and smoothing his shirt before he goes on live. The other man checks the batteries in his camera and in the lights and finishes by hooking some wires together before turning the power on. The red light on the camera glows, indicating that it's ready for use.

Marc's business partner Greg walks in. Greg has a bright smile and is feeling optimistic about the day. *He knows what's about to happen.*

"Are you guys ready for the grand opening?" Greg asks with his big smile.

They look at him with skepticism but reply, "Yep, we're ready."

Marc's family follows him in. None of them want to miss the first day of business. While this is Marc's first restaurant, Greg graduated from Siena College with a degree in Business and Marketing and ran a successful business for twelve years.

The morning quickly comes to an end bringing the first lunch business. It's twelve noon. As four people open the door and enter the restaurant the bell above rings. They sit down. Three more walk in, they sit down. Another group of people walk in; the restaurant slowly comes to life. The wait staff does their best to greet and seat the customers. Marc's Mom hands out menus to guests and his stepfather goes into the kitchen to help make sandwiches. His sisters are behind the bar helping people with coffee and answering questions when all of a sudden, just seven minutes after noon, chaos breaks loose. Thirty people flood through the front door, bell jingling wildly. Accompanying the Mayor of Schenectady are a few local politicians, a journalist from the local newspaper, and his photographer, and yet another local TV news reporter from Albany, Channel 10.

The restaurant is packed in an instant and is overflowing with customers, cameras, lights, news crews, and journalists. There's little room for the wait staff to perform their duties. Plates clink, silverware falls, and tingle on the floor and the bell over the door keeps ringing. The servers serve, the bartenders pours, and there's the rich scent of coffee brewing. Sixteen different flower arrangements arrive with cards wishing "good luck" and "much success." The noise level rises with everyone's conversations. Madonna's, "*Ray of Light,*" plays in the background.

The original TV crew only now seems to realize why they were called to this grand opening and bustle over to Greg, nearly toppling him. As both news stations compete for face time, Greg finds himself in the middle of a media scrimmage. Both local TV stations and the newspaper reporter ask questions: "Did you expect all of this business on your first day?", "What were your expectations?" and "Do you have any other business plans for the future?" Greg satisfies their inquiries and the camera crew turns to the Mayor. "Will there be more new businesses opening," they eagerly ask. "Do you have an overall plan for the revitalization of Schenectady?"

Meanwhile, more people flow in. The hanging bell on the door rings constantly. Guests are curious and excited, happy and smiling. Everyone stops to wish the owners well. Very quietly the Hispanic woman who was sitting at the bar before lunch approaches the kitchen looks in at Marc and asks, "Do you need any help?" Her voice is soft but with a strong Spanish accent. "My name is Maria. I wait tables, make drinks, and clean very well," she says. "I read your menu and I can start now, its *muy loco* in here!"

Marc jumps at the opportunity, grabs a check pad for Maria and hands it to her. He shakes her hand, smiles, and exclaims, "Welcome to Ambition."

We set our expectation on grossing about $110 our first day; we netted $1,600. We had no idea 170 people would come in for lunch on our first day of business. We also thought a staff of three people would be able to handle a lunch crowd. We made a lot of mistakes that first day, simple things like not having enough rolled coins. (Who knew?) Although we had our hopes, we never thought Ambition would come out of the gate charging. Who would've thought that Schenectady would embrace an openly gay owned restaurant? On that day, we found out exactly what Schenectady wanted. Two guys, one dream, and a restaurant called Ambition.

I'm Marc Renson, the co-owner, founder, creator, head chef, waiter, bartender, pot washer and handyman of Ambition all in one. Like a pastry shell to a pie, I hold Ambition together. Yes, I wear many hats—I have to, I own a restaurant. When discussing the idea prior to opening people often admire the idea. "So you want to own a restaurant?" they ask. "It's going to be a lot of fun." It does seem fun and those are the first words out of everyone's mouth. *They were mine.*

I was approached by another restaurant owner who said to me, "It's great to own your own restaurant. You only have to work half a day."

I sighed, said, "Whatever," and waved him away.

He laughed and insisted that it was true. "Just pick the twelve hours a day you want to work!"

Now. Welcome to my world. Sit back, get comfortable, and enjoy a fresh cup of coffee. Every day in Schenectady is a journey: sometimes it's a trip to see the Wizard, sometimes *A Nightmare on Jay Street*, and sometimes it's *Alice's Adventures in Wonderland*. Schenectady is a pretty hard town. Among the hardworking people of this city are the meek and mildly insane. There are numerous mental health clinics, and various drug and alcohol programs here to help and we're here to help too. Ambition is never boring and never the same thing twice.

I'll take you behind the scenes at my restaurant and lead you to the other side of the counter as I wait on the guests. You'll have first-hand knowledge of running my restaurant on any given day. You'll know the problems that occur, the people that I meet and all the craziness that happens. Drama, dysfunction, and a magical dose of divine intervention—that's how I like to sum it up.

In a world of uncertainty, I want to give you the truth about Ambition. The story that way is stranger (and funnier) than any fiction. Throughout my daily experiences at work I often hear myself saying, "This is insane. This is from the pages of a book," or "This isn't supposed to happen for real," It does.

Every day, people find new and *ummm...* interesting questions to ask: "Is there milk in the cream of tomato soup?" "What does vanilla tea taste like?" Or the ever-popular, "Are you open?" The sign reads closed and the lights are off. If someone asked you, "What's in the potato, beer and cheese soup?" Aside from the wonderful experience that it's been, it's these questions and the wonderful patrons who asked them that inspired me to write this book. What would you tell them when they ask? How am I supposed to respond? Especially when they ask me, "Is the coffee fresh?"

I officially started collecting notes in 2002, when my good friend, George, made it simple for me, "This is a book. Write everything down." For two years I jotted down all the craziness that was said on napkins, sugar packets, coffee cups, guest checks, register tape, anything. Before I knew it, I had paper everywhere and finally decided to sift through it all. In between running Ambition, maintaining a home, caring for two very demanding dachshunds (Oscar & Lucy), birthdays, holidays, vacations, weddings, funerals and keeping my personal relationship afloat, it took two years to type this all out, and without the twice-a-day help of Geritol.

CHAPTER 2

AMBITION
coffee house and eatery

Is The Coffee Fresh?

This book officially takes its name from a customer named Tim who asked me every day for months, "Is the coffee fresh?" He walks in. We see him coming. We give a communal sigh and put on our smiles. He sidles up to the bar and asks, "Is the coffee fresh?" *Would he ask this at Starbucks?*

Tim is a quirky kind of guy with thinning blonde hair, blue eyes, and he's a little on the chunky side. He's a simple man with simple taste. His pants are always four sizes too big and scrunched up under the cinch of a belt he wraps under his belly. Most of the time his shirt is almost all the way tucked in.

We answer, "Yes, Tim, the coffee is fresh." After all, Ambition is, among other things, a coffee house. This little back and fourth of ours went on for about six months before I finally snapped. One day, in comes Tim. He slowly paces towards the bar, stares blankly at me, with his question at the ready. With those big blue eyes of his staring directly into mine, suddenly the world went into slow motion. He opened his mouth and out it came: "Is the coffee fresh?"

The world now spins faster. I recite four "Hail Mary's" and reached for the counter to hold on. I've told him yes a hundred times. I opened my mouth and out it came: "No, Tim. None of it is fresh"

Caught of guard, Tim steps backward to catch his balance, blinks and tries again. "And what about your special feature, is that fresh?"

"No, Tim," I said. "None of it is fresh. It's all stale. It's all been here since yesterday." Tim considered it for a moment and, without buying a coffee, he plodded out of Ambition. I didn't care that I just lost a customer, I was tired of being asked, is the coffee fresh.

About two weeks later who walks in again, none other than our buddy with part of his shirt hanging out. But this time, he doesn't ask, "Is the coffee fresh?" He just orders a large cup of coffee, as simple as that. I'm amazed that he actually learned from the situation. Tim still comes in and to this day he'll glare those blue eyes at me and say with a smile, "Is the coffee fresh?"

Now that he's done asking us if the coffee is fresh, my good friend now comes armed with an overwhelming amount of trivial questioning and asks, "Who do you like better, Duran Duran or The Thompson Twins?"

I pick The Thompsom Twins because, Tim, you need a "*Doctor, Doctor!*"

Maria chooses Duran Duran. "*Senor*, Marc, do you know I chose Duran Duran?"

"Yah, Maria, because he's crazy like the wolf."

Maria is my Spanish good luck charm. She's gracious but has a sharp tongue, especially in Spanish. She's very religious, and is deathly afraid of bad omens, lightening, ghosts, and superstitions. She drives me nuts but I adore her. I guess we have that special relationship that few people share.

As customers come in the restaurant, Maria will scan them and if she feels they're shady she'll turn her big brown eyes in my direction, and give me that "look" of something's up. I send out my little energy arrows and I start seeing images in the person's aura. Oh, forgot to tell you, I'm psychic. That too Maria has a problem with. "Oh, *Senor* Marc, that's black magic," she'll say. So I have to admit I will sometimes, and of course just sometimes tell her about what she did last night or what she'll be doing later in the day and Maria will hold her hands up to her ears and out loud say Spanish la-la-la-la-la's!

Snapping at Tim was the day I finally got the message, so to speak I'm supposed to write a book. Something clicked inside and triggered a thought. Without Tim, there might not have been a book. *My hat comes off to you, Tim, and I take a bow.* As I look back on many things in my life and the people who were sent before me whether it being a good or a bad situation, those people were there for a reason. Just like Maria, sitting at the bar on my first day of business. These interventions come at times when I need them the most but least expect them.

I'm standing in the kitchen when I hear the bell on the front door jingle and suddenly I smell daisies. My first reaction is yelling to Maria, "Yo-*loco* easy on the perfume!" Then suddenly I realize who it is.

Maria comes around the corner, "Did you call me Senor Marc?" And she stops. "Ooooh-no, not again." Maria then said something in Spanish so fast and softly under her breath I can't make it out. She quickly walked away. So I go out to the counter to help Fancy Alice.

Now I know Alice. She's been in before. I also know she owns a floral shop which explains why she smells like daisies. When she's medicated, her blonde hair is neatly groomed. Today it's pulled back tight in a bun and she almost looks Japanese. The heavy application of eyeliner only adds to her Asian look. She also sticks baby's breath in her hair. I think the baby's breath touch is a bit much but I'm not the one walking around with weeds in my hair so more power to you—she is fancy Alice and in comes Alice. "Do you have iced coffee?"

"Yes, we do. We have our house blend, which is already chilled, but if you want anything other than that we can ice it down for you."

When a customer orders coffee, you would think they'll know what it's going to taste like. Of course there are many different flavors. The Italian roasts are generally dark and smoky. Columbian is generally mild. Sumatra is generally dark, smooth with a buttery finish. All in all though, you just know what coffee is going to taste like. Or at least *we* think you do.

"What does the iced coffee taste like?"

Unable to find any other explanation, I explain that it tastes like coffee, but it's cold. She didn't seem satisfied. I could have asked if she knew what a mango tastes like. I could have proceeded to explain that iced coffee doesn't taste like a mango. Satisfied or not, Alice decided on the pre-chilled house blend, fixed her coffee and left.

On Alice's heals, in came the twins. Oh, the twins. (And I don't mean what you guys are thinking about right now. Get your minds out of the gutter for a little while at least.) These particular twins who like to flavor their coffee, which is fairly coffee-drinker chic these days. Some days they like to sprinkle cinnamon or nutmeg. Other days they like a syrup to make it taste like caramel or raspberry.

I think parents play cruel jokes on twins by dressing them up in matching clothes as kids. Well, thirty years later, here come Tina and Toni, still in pink: pink pants, pink shoes, pink jackets and their hoods are up so we can see the full effect of pink with of course the faux fur around their hoods. The only person who's happy here is Molly Ringwald. She's not being called, *Pretty in Pink*, anymore.

Have you ever tried waiting on twins? Toni gives me their orders, which are two coffees with caramel flavoring. Then Tina changes her mind and wants a caramel latte. So of course, that sounds delicious to Toni so she changes her mind and orders a chocolate cappuccino.

"Mmmm," says Tina, "that sounds good. Can I have caramel and chocolate in my latte?" So of course the floodgates are now wide open.

In my mind, I hear my guides yelling, "Tsunami!"

Toni comes back with, "Yeah, and can I have caramel in my chocolate cappuccino too?" Meanwhile, my head is like a ping-pong ball, back and fourth, back and fourth. "Oh, but you know what, I want whipped cream on mine," says Tina.

"Yeah, why not, just put whipped cream on mine too," says Toni.

Finally there's silence! I hear Enya's *"Sail Away"* playing in my mind as I slip into a fast meditation relieving myself of the chaos that just happened. They both stand still in front of me staring as if I just pressed pause on a remote. Meanwhile, I'm just trying to absorb the information. *I should look into getting a human remote. Pause, rewind, play... and mute would come in handy. Let's rewind this scene until they're back out the door, then press scene skip and fast-forward.*

"Are you ladies sure now?" I ask.

"Oh yeah, we're sure." They both say in perfect concession. "How much is that going to cost?" Tina asked.

I turn around and look at the coffee board with the prices that are clear as day, pointing and saying out loud, "Espresso, two shots of syrup, and whipped cream." I add them up and recite the price.

Both girls are jolted as if lightening just struck them. "Ooooh, that's too much money, I'll just have a small coffee," says Tina.

"Yeah, me too," says Toni.

Maria's peeking around the corner pointing and giggling. *It's so much funnier when it's at someone else's expense.*

What did I do to deserve this? Maybe I was a twin in a past life and now my karma is coming back around ten fold. At any rate, they always say things come in three's. Hidden behind the twins and now next in line is a gentlemen. Maria comes from around the corner and asks, "Can I help you?"

"Yes, what does the vanilla tea taste like?"

Maria is witty and quick on her feet but she passed this one to me. "*Senor* Marc, what does the vanilla tea taste like?" She's ready to laugh. I don't respond. She looks back at the gentleman and says, "Think vanilla yogurt, think vanilla pudding, think vanilla cookies. This is a simple thing. It will taste like vanilla." *We're not launching the shuttle--it's just tea.*

New guests arrive and Maria goes off to greet her next table and comes back. She looks a little wound up. She has that look like she been asked that question again. And that's exactly what happened. "Why do customers ask is it good? The vegetable medley soup, "is it good?" The sandwich special, "is it good?" Do they think I'm going to tell them no? I should tell them no! The soup tastes like shit and the 'special of the day,' is disgusting!"

Maria now has a few tables she's waiting on and at table #9 a single woman ordered her lunch and told Maria she was allergic to Cajun spices. She then proceeded to order our rajun cajun sandwich—grilled chicken breast, muenster cheese, mayo, lettuce, tomato, bacon with *Cajun spices* on sourdough bread. Now this college scholar asked Maria, will the Cajun spices bother me? Maria automatically answered, "Yes, the Cajun spices will bother you, if you're allergic to them." *I'm thankful Maria's so smart and able to answer such questions for guests.*

She comes back to the kitchen and hands me the order and says, "Crazy *lady at table #9.*"

We make *gelato*. "Gelato" means ice cream in Italian. There are many different flavors, textures, and colors of *gelato*. Strawberry is red, but so is raspberry. Vanilla is white and so is coconut. Peach is a shade of orange but then again orange crème is too. So we decorate each according to its flavor to minimize confusion: strawberries on the strawberry *gelato*, raspberries on the raspberry *gelato*, and so on. Nevertheless, we're often asked what flavor is the one with the strawberries on it. And the *gelato* with the raspberries on top, what flavor is that?

A mother and her child are standing before me at the gelato case and the mother asked me, "What's the green one with the brown chocolate chips?"

Just then the daughter said, "Its mint chocolate chip, Mommy." *I find myself often wondering who's teaching whom.*

Here's a question for you, the reader: the white one with the lemon on top, what flavor is that? *Come in to Ambition and test your IQ.*

As summer rolls around, we like to make cold soups to keep things fun and exciting for the guests. Maria had a new table, so she walked over and greeted them. Maria is originally from Queens, which is where *a little bit* of her personality comes from. She walked over to the table, "*Hola*, how are you two today? Our soup today is a cool cantaloupe with a strawberry rum swirl. The lunch special is mango chicken salad in a spinach wrap with lettuce, tomato, red onions and candied pecans. Can I start you both with a beverage?" They both ordered lemonade.

Maria brings the beverages back to the table and the woman asked, "Is there cantaloupe in the soup?"

"No, we used corned beef, but we call it cantaloupe," Maria answered. Then smiled and said, "*Si*, Marc did use cantaloupe in the soup." She later tells me her experience at this table and I, of course, jot down all my notes.

The next day I made a coconut pineapple cream. I told the wait staff to sell it as tasting like a piña colada. Unlike yesterday, today I added, yes, there is real pineapple in the soup. *We didn't get any questions that day regarding soup. I like to think we removed all doubt.*

How would you advise my employees to answer a question of this caliber: Does your cream of tomato soup have milk in it?

No, it doesn't. That white stuff pouring out of the milk container is just soup softener to keep it fluffy.

How about the cream of mushroom soup; does that have milk in it? *If I answer, no, it has cream in it, would that satisfy them? Hmmm, I'll have to try it.*

I don't know what it's like in other cities or other coffee houses, but cost is the biggest determinant here in Schenectady. *How much does that cost?* I think that if it's something you want, get it. The cost shouldn't be a factor. We're talking about muffins and scones here, not automobiles.

Did you know that when you order something that creates more labor or that costs more to make, it increases the price? Say, for example, a car with a sunroof will cost more than a car without a sunroof. Do we all agree on that?

We had a young lady in Ambition who wanted an egg white omelet. We make omelets using three eggs. Egg *white* omelets, we use five eggs, taking the *time* to separate the yolk from the white. There's an increase in price for using *more* eggs and *more* labor, which increases the overall food cost of the item. One young lady just couldn't understand why an egg white omelet would cost more. As she said, "It's only half the egg. Like, why does it cost more?" She then turned to her friend, from whom she expected agreement. Fortunately, her friend understood basic mathematical concepts.

I've always been told it's good to have choices, but giving customers a choice when ordering an egg sandwich in the morning is a real battle—*we're talking Gettysburg here.* A person would need to know what it is they want on their egg sandwich before even beginning to form a sandwich. Let's see, do I want egg, sausage and cheese on a bagel? Or do I want egg, bacon and cheese on a croissant? This is pretty tough, I know, but this is the curve—we ask what kind of cheese they would like on their egg sandwich. "What usually comes on it?" one woman asked.

"It's your sandwich," I replied, "you tell me. What kind of cheese do you like?"

"I don't know. Maybe American cheese?" *The confetti and balloons went everywhere for me when she answered that question.*

Stacy is another one of our waitresses. She's a brunette with blue eyes and curvy in all the right places—she's easy on the eyes. Stacy works on Wednesday mornings. We have more male customers on Wednesday's then any other day. I wonder why…*boobs!*

One of Stacy's customers demanded that her latte be extremely hot. Then the woman proceeded to let it sit for ten minutes before she drank it. So Stacy asked her if her latte was hot enough and she replied, "I haven't tried it yet."

"Brilliant," she said sweetly and with a smile. So she said to me, "Now Marc, I'm no scientist, but time and temperature, there's some kind of connection." *It's a no-win situation.* Just like the old timers in that diner whose soup was just never hot enough. It could be boiling as you walk it over to the table with a smoke line coming out of it like a window at a bingo hall, but the soup still isn't hot enough.

With the advent of Starbucks, the TV shows *Friends* and *Seinfeld.* We've been introduced to the sometimes-funny world of modern coffees. Gone are the days when you walked in and ordered a regular cup of coffee (originally meaning coffee with milk and two sugars.) Today it's a double short shot of decaf espresso, skinny, yet tall, with dry froth and sprinkle of cinnamon. Even I need a dictionary to understand the myriad of options. Essentially, coffee drinking has become an extension of a chemistry class. It's all weights and measures. Coffee should one day appear on the periodic table of elements and have its place in a high school science curriculum.

Another day slowly comes to a close. It's 5:30 p.m. the floors are mopped, the register is counted, cups and napkins are restocked for tomorrow's business and I'm ready to leave.

I walk out to my Jeep and start driving up Union Street. I pass Union College on my left and continue driving. As I'm about to pass my dentist's office (*my pain-free, thank Jesus, hallelujah, dentist!*) Dr. Schwartz (*he's a nice Jewish boy!*) I see a man pushing a shopping cart filled with empty cans and bottles. I assume he's on his way to the local food store to cash in on his rewards. He's on my right side, on the shoulder of the road, pushing his cart. He's African-American and about 60 years old, give or take a few years. As I drive around him I wonder where he's collected all those cans, and how long it took him. Then I think about his lifestyle. *I'm not sure if I'd want to be the one on the side of the road pushing a shopping cart filled with empty cans. Maybe I'm too vain?* I now recognize and hear Tracy Chapman singing "*Fast Car*" playing on the radio. *Umm, that's weird.* As I'm driving, I'm thinking of all the things I have that he probably doesn't. Then I think about all my cans and bottles at the restaurant and I think if I ever see him in downtown on Jay Street I will give him my bottle returns. The thought makes me smile. I continue driving up Union Street and soon I no longer see the man or his shopping cart in my rearview mirror. And it's almost like it never happened. My thoughts move quickly on to other ideas.

CHAPTER 3

And the Day Begins

Buzz, buzz, buzz! Oh, come on! Sounds my alarm then the music follows. I hear Stephanie Mills singing "*Never Knew Love like This Before.*" I reach over and hit the snooze button, looking at the blinking time—6:00 a.m. and its silent... for nine minutes. *Buzz, buzz, buzz!* Oh, shut up, I think. Now I hear the disc jockeys talking some nonsense about last night's reality TV show. I glance over at the blinking time again—6:09am. I hit snooze. Screw it. *Buzz, buzz, buzz!* By the third round, I wake up immediately. Madonna's song "*Borderline*" is playing. *This song is a get-your-butt-out-of-bed mantra to me.*

Now, it's 6:21 a.m. and I start my morning ritual. I brew the coffee, take a shower, and then pick clothes out of the dryer because last night I failed to finish the laundry—pretty typical for me. I choose a black wrinkled Neil Diamond concert T-shirt from his last tour, grab my Calvin jeans, jacket, and I'm out the door by about 6:45 a.m.

I arrive in the parking lot at 6:56 a.m., the start of my day. Sandwiched between now and closing time at 5:00 p.m. This a day that's stressful, hysterically funny at times (even when people don't mean it to be), emotional and completely unpredictable. I park my Jeep.

After I cross this parking lot behind Ambition, in front of me is an alleyway that connects to the pedestrian walkway, Jay

Street. There's a red-bricked building along side this alleyway, on my right, known for being rented to prostitutes, drug dealers, and other such desirables. It's a typical city street in an urban area and subject to all the problems that this can bring. There are overflowing garbage cans, a broken bike, and an abandoned shopping cart. There's no shortage of empty liquor bottles in brown bags left from the night before. As I continue, I see pigeon poop on the ground in desperate need of cleaning and more garbage blowing in the morning wind. It's cool, as fall is here in the northeast. I can see my breath. My hands are in my pockets to keep them warm, and I feel for my keys, getting ready to unlock the door. I keep walking and take a right around the corner of this fine housing facility. I'm now on the beautiful red-bricked walkway called Jay Street.

The yellow autumn mums that decorate the street are fighting hard, but losing their battle against Mother Nature as fall turns to winter. The leaves on the trees are turning beautiful colors of red, orange, and yellow, and then, there she is, Ambition. She's nestled into the bottom floor of a beautiful old building constructed in 1870—stamped right on the cornerstone. We recently repainted the facade a pale yellow with dark blue trim and white accents. There's a tin awning over the top window on her right side, which is painted brick red to match the great brickwork on her left. As I look up, our sign hanging above the door is swinging and squeaking in the wind. I put the key in the lock, turn it full circle and push the door open.

The smell of coffee hits me. *Isn't that a great smell in the morning?* It's dark as I enter, and the *beep-beep* of the security system sounds faintly. I walk down the entry aisle past the six booths on the right, and disengage the security system. The beeping stops and it's silent again. I walk to the thermometer and turn the heat up from sixty degrees to sixty-eight. I turn right and go behind the bar. The slapping of the old wooden pallets underneath the rubber mats can be heard hitting the floor with each step I take. I flip the lights on behind the bar and turn the espresso machine on. It beeps, circulates water, and then starts its heating process. I turn on both our air pot and dual coffee brewer. I reach behind the coffee thermos and turn on the coffee station track lighting. In the kitchen, I switch on yet another bank of lights. I'm looking around at everything, the grill, sinks and sandwich cooler, making sure everything looks untouched, unbroken, and ready to go. One of the *great* rewards of owning my own business is I get to deal with any problem that has occurred over night—luckily, nothing this time.

I grab my candle lighter, open the oven door, light the pilot, and fire it up so we're ready to bake. (We have a circa 1970 South Bend stove/grill which operates like a champ, but needs a bit of coaxing, love and attention to spring to life.) Next I light the flattop. Now the whole grill is on. I turn on my hood fans and put my garbage can in place. I unwrap the croissants that are proofing (a term used for the rising of dough) then step out of the kitchen, allowing time for the oven to preheat. I begin grinding the coffee.

My morning ritual is well underway by the time I start baking the bagels, blueberry scones, apple turnovers and croissants. I also bake chocolate chip and peanut butter cookies. What a great aroma of flavors mixing together in the morning. The scent of coffee brewing with the baking of cinnamon and sugar from the pastries, all mixing with the scent of warm chocolate from the cookies. I grab eggs from the walk-in cooler and the milks for the coffee station. I start cooking the bacon. It's now about 7:40 a.m. and I stop to refill my own coffee. I breathe, sip, and sip again. I wonder what's going to happen today that will be different from yesterday? *Poof!* Just like that, I remember hearing Madonna sing earlier. The thought left as quickly as it came.

I walk back behind the bar and turn on the must-have music. I load my early morning selections. This particular morning, *Joshua Kadison* is singing *"Jessie"* from his CD *Painted Desert Serenade.* This puts a smile on my face and a song in my heart. I try to figure out why Jessie the character in the song doesn't love him back, but I guess it could be many things. I love story songs. And most of Joshua's songs are little stories.

Now it's 7:55 a.m. and in walks Maria. We say good morning usually (if I'm in a good mood). Mornings for me are semi-sweet but not exactly like the chocolate. After all these years of waking up early one would think I would be used to it. I'm not. (One of my lunch entrees took its name from my morning self, Crabby Marc.) *I can poke fun at myself. I mean why not, my staff does.* So, depending on the day, Maria and I smile, nod, or say nothing at all. We'll save the pleasantries for later on when I'm above water and ready to face the world. We do our last-minute duties and push out Luigi, our over-weight, chubby-cheeked, smiling, life-size chef statue holding our blackboard of daily specials. I flip the rest of the lights on, turn the "closed" sign around and the day begins.

I journal my thoughts so, throughout the day, I write down anything that stands out. Hearing Madonna sing *"Borderline"* goes on a piece of paper and into my pocket. These are my *little signs* so when the day is over I journal all of them and I review the ways that the Universe communicated with me. *I know, you're thinking, he's a freak!* Doing this taught me that when I hear *"Borderline"* early in the morning I know to get a move on. In the afternoon if I hear the song I know it's just playing on the radio. It carries no information. Music is my connection with the Universe. Certain songs will play, and me knowing that lyrics carry meanings *for me*. I know I'm supposed to hear that song at that time to prepare me for what awaits ahead.

This day seems to be going along like any other day. I often neglect to pay attention to my *sign*. When that happens, I drop my guard and then just out of the sky drops a problem. The phone rings. Maria answers: "Okay, I'll tell him." She hangs up. "Marc," she tells me, "Danny just called out!" Danny is my kitchen helper. He's a young kid, reliable most of the time… except for today. Little did I know, today would be the day I needed him the most. Its 10:15 a.m.

An hour later, and like a penny from the roof of a building, drops another problem. The phone rings again. Maria answers, writes down some things, writes down some more things, turns the page on her note pad and writes down some more. Just watching her do this, I get anxious. Why is she writing so much, what's going on. The control freak in me goes off and I walk over to where Maria is and I see her notes. I'm getting angry now. What the hell is this, I wonder. Who waits until 30 minutes to noon to place a take-out order for 18 people, then wants it ready for pick-up in thirty minutes? Do I say, no, sorry we can't help you, and lose their business? We're not a bank; restaurants don't have the luxuries of knowing people will wait. I don't switch banks because tellers are slow but I would like to. (As I stand there waiting in line for a teller and the person behind me is tapping their foot, *tap,tap,tap,tap,tap*. Followed by the heavy exhale, that exaggerated sigh, like they just held their breath for two minutes, and it hits me in the back of the neck.)

But customers *will* leave a restaurant—no one likes to wait for food. They might leave Ambition and go to another restaurant that will service their needs when they need them if we don't provide service right then and there. Today's lunch needs will not be given to me again tomorrow. I'm given an opportunity to capitalize on unexpected business.

Now, if this 18-person lunch order was the only thing I had going on today that would've been great. (Imagine... I'm opening my doors at lunch to feed 18 people and then go home. What a perfect day!) But this isn't perfect right now, I'm going to be all alone in the kitchen feeding however many people come through my door as well as this unexpected take out party. Just then it happened. Another problem dropped out of the sky. The health inspector walks in...F***! I stand there fisting my hands in anger. This is another one of those moments when the world absolutely stops. Seeing the health inspector walk in is like getting that call from the police telling you your child was in a car accident. There's nothing but anxiety and questions going through my mind. Did I clean the meat slicer? Yes. Is everything labeled and dated in the walk-in refrigerator? Yes. Did the wait staff put hand towels and fill the hand soap dispensers in the bathrooms? Yes. Did I put the eggs back on the bottom shelf? Yes. But every possible worse-case scenario goes through my mind and I've got to get this massive lunch order ready to go out in 15 minutes.

Welcome, reality. I have no help in the kitchen with the 18 sandwiches and now the health inspector asks me to "take a walk." *Great! Let me spin around into Wonder Woman make 18 sandwiches and then tip-toe through the tulips with the health inspector.* Meanwhile, other food tickets are piling up in the kitchen. This entire fiasco is going down. And going down fast! Like the plane spiraling down from the sky, so too is my world at this moment. I want to cry. I want to scream! Why me! Why now! I have so many emotions going through me right now all I can do is ask the universe for just a little help.

As I shake, tears filling my eyes, I swallow hard, and I just don't know what to do. Then, all of a sudden, I look down. At the exact moment there's a white feather on the floor. And, in that exact instant, in all my chaos, as quick as this all started, I felt hope. I felt some sort of feeling come over me as I heard the bell on the front door ring. I looked towards the door through my whirlwind of emotions and there, walking in, is Jeremy, a kitchen employee of mine with a great big smile on his face.

"My eleven o' clock class was cancelled." He looks around and says, "Wow. You're busy. Do you need some help?"

"Jeremy," I said, "you have no idea, how much I need you right now! Absolutely, please go in the kitchen and hold the fort down while I walk around with the health inspector." As I point to the man holding his clip board.

"Ooohhh," says Jeremy. He does his fastest at dropping his back pack, pulling off his designer T-shirt, while working in his white undershirt and grabbing for his baseball hat.

"Maria," I yell, "Make sure he sees the to-go order!" She nods.

I walked around with the inspector. He found one thing he didn't like—a single fluorescent bulb didn't have a plastic covering on it which in the event the light bulb is broken, the plastic covering would contain the glass.

I go back in the kitchen with Jeremy and we finish the lunch business and it's a total success. Jeremy showing up, the take out order goes out effortlessly, all the guests are happy and I had an almost perfect health inspection. As I see it, it is a perfect inspection. No dirtiness, no cross contamination, all my temperatures were up to snuff. The inspector left happy and I returned to a happier state-of-mind.

As I look back on the situation, all I did was put my feelings aside and ask for a little help. Ask and it will be given. And it all started this morning with Madonna singing.

CHAPTER 4

Inside Ambition

Welcome to Ambition. As you enter, you'll notice immediately it's not your average coffee house. I'm not even sure myself what Ambition is at times. Is she a restaurant? A coffee house? A bar? An art studio? What I can say with absolute certainty is she's original. The restaurant is ninety feet deep, and the widest point is 28 feet across, which is the bar area. We have local artwork on the walls that is changed every two months. Silver wall sconces and hanging silver light fixtures add to the room's authenticity. In 1908, a restaurant named Twentieth Century Lunch owned by Asbury B. Christian laid the white and green Greek mosaic tiling on the floor, which has aged with a few cracks but still beautiful. The ceilings are the original tin ceilings painted white and in good condition, considering the years that have passed since installation. The walls are painted golden-rod yellow and hunter green. The booths are burgundy. There are six booths as you walk in on your right with the original call buttons for the waitresses. (These are doorbells that "ding" when pressed, letting the servers know they're wanted and *yes*, they still work.) We painted the support poles, radiators and the heating ductwork burgundy to keep the color theme running through the restaurant. Halfway back, we have a beautiful old telephone booth from the 1950's. (Little inside story: Someone from

Verizon said they needed to remove the phone and the phone booth because Verizon owned both. Since the phone wasn't getting enough use, they said they needed to take them both. I'm a little smarter than the average bear and said, "I own that phone booth because it was in the sale contract. You can take the phone if Verizon needs to, but not the phone booth." So whomever this person was tried, but didn't succeed in stealing the phone booth.) To your left is our beautiful, 1944 bar. This was installed by Eddie Karwan, owner of The Jay Tavern. It has a glossy mahogany finish with rounded wood etchings and mirrors.

My kitchen is next. It's the size of most people's closet. It has a stove, a three bay sink, a produce sink, a sandwich cooler prep station and some shelves, but that's it. It's small, but this little room is the beating heart of Ambition. The exact measurements are nine foot nine inches by nine foot nine inches.

Sysco, our food distributor/provider, saw the space before we opened, a closet-sized room for a kitchen with hanging wires, dirt, dust and grease housed in an old run-down building. A year after we were open, Sysco told me they gave us six months and we'd be out of business. As I later learned, taking into account the size of the kitchen and restaurant, Sysco uses a square foot percentage calculation to determine what volume of food per hour we could produce relative to our seating capacity and target serving time. They told me this after we had been open one full year in 2001. We now have a gold account status with Sysco and produce over four times what their little calculation projected us to do in our first year alone. Everybody seems to know how to run my restaurant. (You'll understand my meaning later when you read about the advice customers offer because obviously if they owned Ambition, this is how they would operate it. *What are opinions like…?*)

Everyone loves my bell. We have a counter bell given to me by my late Aunt Pinky. This bell sits on our food counter right outside the kitchen door. While my aunt was at a hospital battling Multiple Sclerosis her bed call button didn't work, so the nurses gave her this bell to "ding" when she needed assistance. When the hospital did fix the call button, my aunt gave me the bell for the restaurant. So I now bug the hell out of the wait staff by ringing it. *"Ding-ding, pick up your food, ding-ding!"* Customers come in and "ding" the bell, something so small yet so much fun. Thank you, Aunt Pinky. I lost my aunt January 3, 2006, so with a smile in my heart, I say, "This one is for you, Aunt Pinky. *Ding-ding!"*

Now, past my little kitchen, on the way to the lounge, is my Mom's Hoosier cabinet. It fits perfectly in the restaurant, an antique with a dated metal tag of completion from 1906. In the lounge we encounter another of my mother's pieces, a Coca Cola tin policeman. It was used in school zones back in the 1950s. It's a cop holding up a "slow school zone" sign. We have him all dazzled up with a feather boa, shiny silver hair and Mardi Gras beads. *He looks fabulous.*

We installed hardwood floors in the back to make it cozier. We have an old but functional safe that we use as a filing cabinet, two tables for guests, mixed chairs and a purple couch. There's also a camouflaged walk-in cooler. It was an old ugly brown monstrosity, so we painted a mural over it to make it fun and functional. We have Cher, Lucy, Madonna, Cyndi Lauper, Bette Davis, Marilyn and Elvis painted on the cooler's door. We enter the walk-in cooler periodically throughout lunch, and you hear the guests say, "I didn't even see that door there." Well, that's the point.

If you're ever in Ambition in the warmer months and it's nice and cool, thank Gladys. Gladys is our air conditioning unit on top of our walk-in cooler. I was told by Stephanie Karwan, the previous owner that "Gladys" was installed in the 1950's. She's been blowing cold air for over fifty years and with some tender-loving-care she's still working and humming right along with us. *That a girl!*

There's a lot to look at in Ambition. I decided to hang pictures and album covers on the water pipes over the bar to disguise them. There are pictures of all my favorite music celebrities, entertainers, movies, and bottle caps glued to our archway making the wall colorful and sparkly. Guests, when they see something new, ask, "How long has that been there?" (Popular question). Usually the answer is, "Years."

Ambition has spirit energy, which many of the guests feel as soon as they walk in. It's that sense of someone is watching you, but nobody's physically there. Maria was hysterical one day, "I saw someone behind the bar just now with dark hair, a white t-shirt and jeans. It was a man. He was hurrying. It happened so fast that when I looked again there was nobody." Maria has her phobia of ghosts. She grabs two spoons from the kitchen and walks back behind the bar clinking them together. She makes a cross with them and crouches down like a war is about to breakout.

"Maria," I say, "You're giving a new meaning to the show "TAPS." Then I asked her, "What do you think, he's a vampire? Why don't you throw some garlic at him? Maybe that'll chase him away." I never know what to tell Maria other then to take it easy. I do know there's definite spirit energy that we feel and see in this building.

Stacy and I have seen the spirit too. *We've all seen Blackboots.* Stacy went to the door that leads to the upstairs, came back white as a ghost and said, "If I tell you something promise you won't think I'm crazy." She told me she opened the door to the upstairs and there in front of her was a man in black boots. She said she was so scared she didn't look up but just closed the door. A few months later, the upstairs door was open and out of the corner of my eye I saw a pair of black boots walk down the last two stairs. Call us crazy, that's fine, but we know what we saw. Jeremy and Stacy both feel his presence the strongest in the back lounge. We have a light on a pull string in the lounge. The weird thing is this pull-string light will work on the first pull most mornings, but some mornings it takes fifteen to twenty pulls for it to light up. Sometimes it doesn't light up at all, and I have to walk away and come back. Then on the first pull again it will light up.

Jeremy has now been locked upstairs twice by Blackboots. He would go upstairs to get what he needs and as he describes, he's climbing the stairs, he hears the door behind him close and the "flip" of the lock. It's a slide lock. The slide handle has to be physically picked up and slid over to lock the door. He, of course, blamed us the first time. "Some joke guys, ha-ha, funny, funny!" We tried to reason with him saying nobody was around to lock him upstairs and we told him what all of us were doing and how it couldn't have been us. Until it happened again, and this time even Jeremy knew nobody was behind him to lock the door. *Well somebody was behind him.*

I'm completely comfortable anywhere in the building, though some weird things do happen. I'll hear someone cough and I'm the only one in the building. Or something falls that shouldn't, like a light bulb falling out of a hanging fixture. Equipment will just stop or start working. I've heard voices when again I know I'm the only one in the building. The bell on the front door will ring with excitement as if a guest is opening the door, but nobody is actually there, even though the bell itself is *moving.* Or the ever popular blurred movement out of the corners of our eyes. You can try to convince yourself you didn't see anything until it happens again, and then what do you do?

Over the years, many psychics and mediums have come in and they told me identical stories. I've been told there's another spirit, a woman, walking behind me making sure I do things right. Her name is Bula. Now here's a little history about our building. Bula was a madam. The upstairs of Ambition at one time was a brothel. The Law of Attraction states like attracts like. Because of my personality, Bula follows me, guiding, protecting, and yes, sometimes pushing me in the right direction—I'm known to do some pretty stupid things now and then.

I guess Ambition has a soul of her own. She welcomes everyone in. Maybe that's why I'm writing this book. Ambition has a story to tell and wants me to tell it. There are some things we can't explain, and this is one of them. So after you read this book, come and feel Ambition's energy, and tell me about it. I want to know what you feel or see.

I was recently approached by S.T.A.R. Paranormal & Historical Research Team who asked to catch on video paranormal activity in Ambition and use it in their documentary.

I said, "Go for it!"

AMBITION
coffee house and eatery

CHAPTER 5

Just Pick Me a God Damn Sandwich!

It's common to go to a restaurant and ask simple questions like "is the soup homemade," or "is the steak a porterhouse or New York sirloin." These simple questions help us determine if we're going to enjoy our selection. But all too often these simple questions go terribly awry.

Few people walk into a restaurant and don't know what to do. It's a pretty common practice that we either seat ourselves or a host/hostess seats us. So imagine our surprise when guests come in the restaurant and ask a server, "What do you do here?" (Perhaps they're just taking a survey, for they cannot seriously wonder what we are actually doing.) The signs alone should give it away. "See the hostess for seating," for example, should be enough of a clue.

Regarding the nature of the business, again the signs should say it all. As the customers look around the space, taking in everything, there are signs as far as the eye can see: "Place Take Out Orders Here," then the soda coolers, coffee stations, menus, tables, chairs, plates and cutlery and all the food that everyone is eating. *Do they think we get on the bar and dance wildly for everyone?* Is it perhaps a bowling alley, a den of iniquity?

If somebody asked you if the Moroccan *beef* soup was vegetarian, could you resist the obvious answers that might come pouring forth? "No, unfortunately it is made with real Moroccans and therefore it is not vegetarian."

How about this one: "What's your soup today?"

Answer: "Potato, beer, and cheese."

Reply: "What's in it?"

Again, one would have to bite one's tongue not to fall into the obvious, *"Dandelion greens, Yak milk and Spaghetti O's. Any other questions?"*

When ordering tossed salads, restaurants offer a choice of dressings. That's if the salad comes with choices. A Caesar salad, for example, isn't made with anything other than Caesar dressing; hence its name Caesar salad and we all use Caesar dressing. So can you explain to me why we're asked so frequently, what dressings do you have? Dressings for what? Am I missing something here? Does somebody make a Caesar Salad without using Caesar dressing?

We have a section in our menu called "build your own sandwich." When we decided to offer that feature, we never thought people would actually think they had to get up and construct one for themselves. Given the nature of the business, I believe it's pretty clear we'll be more than happy to make your sandwich for you, but you have to tell us what you'd like. That's why I'm in the kitchen and Maria is at your table. We'll be glad to build it for you.

New guests walk in, two women and a five-year-old child. They sit in Jeremy's section. He greets them, brings them menus and tells them the daily specials. Now, innuendos sail over Jeremy's head, but we love him dearly. Jeremy is cute—blonde hair, blue eyes, muscular, and has tattoos. He's "*Candyman*" the Christina Aguilera song. *Jeremy started a wall of notes he's received over the years of men and women wanting him to call them. "Don't miss this opportunity, it won't happen again!" Some people are just so bold and full of themselves. Or desperate?*

So this whole time the woman with the child is smiling at Jeremy, but he thinks nothing of it. Jeremy leaves and comes back over with their beverages. The woman tells Jeremy she wants to build her own sandwich. She started with all her favorites, then she threw in this question, "Are sprouts the things that look like sperm?" she said with a smile and a glint in her eye.

Jeremy calmly answered, "Yes, I guess they do look like sperm. Would you like some on your sandwich?"

"Sprouts or sperm?"

"I'm speaking of sprouts," says Jeremy. "Would you like some sprouts on your sandwich?"

"Neither sprouts nor sperm. Thanks," she replies.

After the woman paid her bill and left, Jeremy cleaned the table and found her phone number on a napkin. "Call me. We can continue our conversation on sperm, Debbie." *I have to wonder if she starred in that movie Debbie Does Dallas? Who knows, maybe she's done Dallas and has moved on to Schenectady?*

Most days I'm in the kitchen prepping the soups, slicing meats and cheeses, making sauces. I'll occasionally take tables on the floor. Being the control freak, I enjoy the kitchen. And of course the kitchen controls the whole restaurant. I don't care how many owners and wait staff a restaurant has; if it doesn't have any cooks, well, you don't have to be psychic to see where I'm going with this one.

So I'm on the floor taking a table and who comes back in, none other than Fancy Alice. I know she's "off her meds" because her hair isn't so neat today. Her lipstick is smeared well around her lips. *Did you look at yourself in a mirror?* And where's the baby's breath, I wonder?

"I can't have nuts! Does your chocolate hazelnut *gelato* have nuts in it?"

"No, Alice," I said, "it's made with peaches."

"Oh, that sounds delicious," she replies. She turns around and walks out.

Thanks for coming in, see you next time. Bye!

Maybe I'm wrong, but I feel the purpose of having an egg white omelet is to avoid the fat of the yolk. *I'm not a nutritionist, just my opinion.* We all know the yolk is fat, so if you take the yolk out, which is the fat, why put more fat in? This concept brings us to diets. We're all on them at some time or another. We all like to think we're proactive in choosing correct low fat items to meet our needs. Then we have the twenty-something girls who are on diets because if a gust of wind can't blow them away, they think they're too fat. And they tell us they're on diets, they order egg white omelets, which is a great choice for a lean breakfast. But then they add green peppers, tomatoes, black olives, extra sausage and Swiss cheese. *Why not just add lard?* Why bother having an egg white omelet? Then they want their dry toast with butter on the side, plus they want half and half and sugar for their coffee. *All in all, an interesting approach to dieting.*

Now we have the guy who wants to build his own sandwich, but reminds you that he's on a diet. So he'll have corned beef, provolone cheese, lettuce, tomatoes, peppers, and carrots on a croissant with low fat mayo, please. Oh yeah, I forgot, he asks you for no pickle, but with extra potato chips. *He must think that as long as low fat mayonnaise was used, the rest of the sandwich just doesn't matter.* Whether he's on the low carb craze or the low fat craze, he just missed the boat on both. But he does have a diet Coke, so he thinks he's on his way to a thinner physique fast.

Irritable Ida and her husband come in and sat at a table. Stacy gives them menus and tells them the specials and leaves them alone for several minutes. Stacy goes back over and Ida's husband knows exactly what he wants. He wants corned beef on rye with Dijon, lettuce, tomato, and onion. Ida on the other hand just can't seem to make up her mind. So Stacy asks, "Do you like turkey?"

"I don't know," replies Ida.

"Do you like roast beef?"

"I don't know," says Ida, getting frustrated, "Just pick me out a God damn sandwich!"

Stacy is a little taken back but smiles and comes back to the kitchen. "Why do I get all the crazies?"

That's right, just take it. No matter how nice we are to some people we have to just take their abuse. Stacy said to me, "I took English as a second language. My first language is Bitch. Bitch, I will punch you in the face!"

Later that afternoon, with the law of attraction working in her favor, Stacy's shift is almost over. Her last customer sat down and ordered a build your own sandwich. Stacy asked him, "What would you like to drink?"

He responded, "None of your damn business!"

I personally thought Stacy was going to pile drive him into the tiled floor. Locking his head between her legs. "There, fool," she'd exclaim, "now it's my business. Let's try this once more, what would you like to drink?"

Size does matter. Don't let anyone fool you. We're constantly asked, "How big is your twenty-ounce coffee? How big is your eight-ounce soup? And how big is your half a sandwich?" This is the restaurant's version of the age old query, "Who is buried in Grant's Tomb?" but we answer as honestly as we can. The twenty-ounce coffee is twenty ounces, the eight-ounce soup is eight ounces, and the half a sandwich is half the size of a full one. *The bells and whistles go off, and I get the grand prize for having all the correct answers. I feel like the winning contestant on The Wheel of Fortune.*

Back in the 80's, Burger King and McDonald's fought it out on how their burgers were cooked, flamed broiled or cooked on a flat top stove. Some of us remember those wars. We had a customer ask, "What make of grill is it and how does it grill?" Who walks into a restaurant and asks that kind of question? Is he comparing grill brands? Sometimes it's just too frustrating to try to figure it all out. We grill the things that can be grilled. We do not grill soup for example. We've also discovered that ice cream doesn't grill well either.

CHAPTER 6

Angels at Work, Creating Ambition and Me

My legal name is Robert Marcel Renson II. I go by the family nickname of Marc. I have short dark brown hair and hazel eyes. I'm 5 foot 8 inches in height with a small build. I mostly wear glasses because I'm too lazy in the morning to put in my contacts. I was born July 17, 1970 and was raised in North Brunswick, NJ until I was fourteen when my family moved to our summer house in Ghent, NY in Columbia County.

I've been with my partner Greg since New Year's Eve, 1998. There's a story there but I'll let my friend Rich Lewis tell it. Like the Go-Go's, *"My Lips Are Sealed."*

And thanks to Mark Walberg, I'll forever be called Marky-Mark. So I'm with you, Mark. I feel your pain. I just don't look as good as you do in Calvin Klein tighty-whities.

My zodiac sign is Cancer the Crab, and I'm true to my sign. I'm protective, I hold emotions in, I don't communicate well, and I'm moody. *And I have a tendency to "snap."*

I don't accept compliments well. I usually find fault in most of my work, so when someone tells me that I did a good job; I usually just say how I could have done it better instead of just accepting the compliment.

I'm definitely a high-energy person with lots of ambition. I put in a solid twelve hours of work a day, six days a week, and writing seven days a week here wouldn't be a stretch. I love coffee, I'm definitely disorganized, but my mess works for me most of the time, I occasionally forget (oops) to pay some bills on time. "Like the light and power bill," says Greg. He laughs and the power company just shuts us off.

I recently lost my American Express card due to my wonderful credit score. One thing I will never care about is that piece of paper with that number or score on it. I refuse to be labeled a number on a piece of paper. You want your American Express card back, here you go! American Express just lost all those late fees and penalties that help keep the company in business. In the 9 years I had that card suddenly they care. My one thousand four hundred dollar charges in a month's time are too much of a risk for a huge billion-dollar corporation like American Express.

I enjoy driving my red 2000 (finally paid off, see I can do it) Jeep Wrangler in the summer with the roof down and the doors off. I have Madonna airbrushed on my spare tire cover, taken from her "*True Blue*" album cover.

I love pop music. Bubble gum pop of the 80's or disco works just fine for me, but music is always around me. In a pinch, I'll even try singing it. I must admit though that I'm not very good. I'll take the radio, a CD, a tape, my iPod or whatever is at hand. One way or another music must always be there.

My parents always played music in the house as we were growing up; mostly disco, because that's what was popular at the time-Captain and Tennille, Cher, Dr. Hook, Donna Summer and Tony Orlando and Dawn to name a few. Paul Anka, Neil Sedaka and Barry Manilow were also slipped in there. Grandma Renson would jump up and swing her hips in a circular motion as she sang, "What's New Pussy Cat?" We would do the Hustle and the Fox Trot in our living room (*as I sit here laughing about it.*) So I believe this is where I got my taste for pop music. My very first album that I bought was *Donna Summer, Bad Girls. Maybe Bula had something to do with me buying that first album? Wouldn't that be fun to know Bula was with me all those years pushing me towards Ambition?* Stranger things have happened.

I'm a spiritualist, and I believe the Universe talks to me, and now I've decided to answer. My writing is an attempt to recognize what I'm doing, bare some of my sins, explain how I feel about those around me and carve out a place for myself.

I believe in the afterlife, guardian angels and the signs that they give to me to interpret to help me along my journey. Things will occur over and over again before I pick up on them. Sometimes I do get them right away and follow their lead. Other times I'm too scattered to pay attention until it finally hits me in the face and says, "Hey stupid, here I am. Pay attention." Sending Tim to ask, "Is the coffee fresh?" one thousand times, for example. Talk about being slow coming out of the starting gate. Could it have been anymore clear? I was tortured with that question for about six months before I realized I'm supposed to write this book. "Why?" you might ask. I really can't say; all I know is the epiphany came and I listened. I mean, come on, how many times could you handle being asked, is the coffee fresh, is the coffee fresh, is the coffee fresh? Before you too, snap and finally pay attention. I listened, and started writing down all the events.

My grandmother passed away in August of 2000. Phil Collins had just put out *"You'll Be In My Heart"*. Shortly after hearing the song something would happen. I would hear the song and Stacy came in looking for a job. I would hear the song again and I found out my mortgage was approved. (*Ta-Daaah!) But I'm sure it had more to do with Greg's credit score. His is well over the 700's.* I heard the song after my mom gave me my grandmother's football sweatshirt for Rutgers. *Born and raised in Jersey, Exit 9, New Jersey Turnpike.* Many, many other instances happened before I realized she, my Grandmother, was communicating with me, which is a pretty cool feeling.

I would get in my Jeep and the song would come on the radio, from start to finish. Without fail something would happen. Sometimes it was good and sometimes not so good. For example, I heard the song as we left on our vacation and the roof leaked from the blocked gutters on our house. The leak collapsed the kitchen ceiling. But the best time was when I was going to bed and turned on the radio just for ten minutes to help calm me down and put me to sleep-and here comes Phil. Oh, boy, I think, and fall asleep wondering. The next day I went to Foxwoods Casino in Connecticut to see Cyndi Lauper in concert and at the show I received a back stage pass to meet her. It's this kind of connection, vibe, gut feeling, instinct, that happens to me all the time. These signs help me get through some pretty tough days, telling me everything is going to be all right. Owning my own restaurant (as all restaurant owners know), everything is *not* always going to be all right. So getting a little help from above, well, that's okay with me.

My grandmother had a picture of herself penciled while she was in Paris, after she retired. Her hair is flawless and she's wearing her mink, and she looks as stately as she was in life. When she passed, I asked my family if I could have that picture of grand mom and got it on one condition, only if I put her next to the bar because she loved her chardonnay. So now, every day, my grandmother is watching me work in the kitchen from her place at the bar.

All my life I've been inspired by movies, Hollywood celebrities, and rock stars.

I enjoyed watching *I Dream of Jeannie*, starring Barbara Eden. After Jeannie, Barbara was in the movie *Harper Valley PTA*, which I just loved. Miss Stella Johnson and her mini skirts. I also watched *Wonder Woman*, *Charlie's Angels*, *The Bionic Woman* and I always loved when *Batgirl* was on *Batman*. It was always the about *the ladies*.

Donna Summer was my first crush. She ruled my world until I was introduced to Cyndi Lauper, (*Sorry Donna!*) I had posters of Donna all over my room, *well I still do*. She helped enforce my love for music with a beat *and a groan!* Donna has had her share of ups and downs and has fought her way back every time. *Donna, thank you for teaching me perseverance and yes Donna, I'm very careful these days of what I wish for.*

I related to Cyndi Lauper, her personality, songs, outfits and wild hair. I was watching the WWF (World Wrestling Federation) and at the time, wrestler Capt. Lou Albano portrayed her father in her video "*Girls Just Want To Have Fun*", then reappeared in her "*She Bop*" and "*Good Enough*" videos, better known as "*The Goonies R Good Enough*". I totally bought right into the whole rock meets wrestling glitz. *Cyndi, I thank you for inspiring me to live a more colorful life.*

Madonna, where do I start? Madonna helped me with my determination. I'm happy to have been able to grow up shall I say with Madonna. She's very brave to have done the things she did as a woman in a man's world. Through it all, the music, videos, crucifixes, being a virgin, burning crosses, crotch grabbing, her "*Sex*" book, *Evita*, and being a mother, Madonna has shown the world this is who she is. She helped teach me to be myself and not to take "No" for an answer. *Madonna, thank you for teaching me how to handle the toughness of this physical world.*

I was only eleven years old when I first saw the movie *9 To 5*. I like Dolly Parton (and still do). Lily Tomlin and Jane Fonda are just brilliant. Dolly's song "*9 To 5*" is still my favorite song of all time. That song and the movie stayed with me all these years. So when we started our business plan, I said, I want to name the restaurant Ambition, taken from Dolly's song. Because that's exactly how I felt and still do. We all work so hard for other people; we never see our own potential. Well, I decided to take the challenge. Thanks to the motivation of the movie and Dolly's song we have a great name for our restaurant. *Dolly, I thank you for your song of inspiration.*

CHAPTER 7

COLLEGE AND WORK

My first job was at a diner. I was just sixteen years old and the year was 1986. Madonna was singing her anthem *"Papa Don't Preach."* George Michael was being banned for his song, *"I Want Your Sex."* Cyndi Lauper was singing *"True Colors."* And we were all watching Dynasty, Knots Landing, The Cosby Show and The A Team. Life and television, for the most part, were good.

I was dishwashing (this is where every person who gets into this business starts). If you don't wash dishes in a restaurant then you won't be in it for life. It's the "you have to crawl before you walk" kind of thing, but what an education. It was there that I discovered all the eccentric people who work in food service. We have the drug users and the dealers. We have the functional drunks who work almost all shift. The sex addicts, and of course, the verbally and physically abusive, throwing pots and pans, knives, hot grease, boiling water and anything else they can get their hands on. Wine glasses work really well. (The competitions at the Roman Coliseum had nothing on a working restaurant!) Then, of course, there are the gamblers. I learned early that you have to watch out for them. Today the owner might be able to pay your salary, but tomorrow is another story. The IRS comes knocking on the door or that horse didn't come in at the Kentucky Derby, and suddenly your paycheck doesn't get signed. Talk about an education—baptism by fire!

It was at this one diner that I found out this was what I want to do with my life. This diner on the Taconic State Parkway in Ghent, NY, back then it was called the Rigor Hill Diner. There I saw for the first time how the rest of the world lived. My parents were good about keeping the real world out of our lives. We had an idea that it was out there but never actually saw it. After I started at the diner, I began seeing the sex, drugs, and drinking, so I also started staying out late. I started using all the swear words I learned from my father. Everyone else was using them. I also saw my first set of tits at this job.

So there I was, sixteen years old, in my white apron, high-top Nike sneakers (unlaced, of course,) Levi's jeans and my Spuds Mackenzie Budweiser t-shirt rinsing off and racking the dirty dishes as the waitresses brought them in. Disquieting the kitchen, in came a waitress who yelled, "Where's my fucking order?"

The line-cook fired back "Shut the fuck up!"

The waitress gracefully said, "Suck on my titties, asshole."

The cook then said, "Yeah, show 'em, bitch."

So the waitress pulled the buttons apart on her shirt uniform and out came the ladies. She grabbed them from underneath and shook them. "Right here, asshole," she said to the cook, and they both started to laugh.

Ah, the joys of working at a diner. When I'm asked what I learned from my first job that's my answer. *Tits.*

I graduated high school—Class of 1989—from Taconic Hills in Claverack, NY. Mom wanted me to go to college. She usually gets her way, from me. After all I'm mommy's little boy! I'm a culinary arts graduate from Schenectady County Community College. I'm dyslexic; I took three years to do a two-year program. Reading and writing are my worst enemies. I would fail all my written tests because I wouldn't read the books. But I would pass my laboratory cooking tests with A's because a hands on style is how I learn. I took three years because I needed to learn. Reading wasn't doing it for me so I jumped on the internship programs that the college offered. I went to Marco Island, Florida and worked at an upscale Resort for four months. (This is some inside information you may not need to know, but I brought a door poster of Madonna (which is life size) from her *Like A Prayer* video. She's in a brown slip, and her hair is dark, and she looks fabulous. Anyway, I cut it out and glued it to a piece of cardboard and drove around with Madonna in the front seat of my car. I, of course, did buckle her in for her safety. I would never want to hurt my Madonna. People always took second looks, as I drove with Madonna all the way to Florida for my internship. That year, 1989, I also took Madonna to our Christmas party, as my date, sitting beside me through dinner. *Oh, I can't believe I just admitted that.* Working in Florida was a nice little wake-up call for what was in store for me in my future of cooking. I started out in *garde manger*, (a far and too fancy way of saying salad prep for the dyslexic tongue). Paula was the manager of this department, and she was known for accidentally dropping her panties to her ankles in the dry storage room. (Dry storage is where cans and paper products are stored.)

I walked into the dry storage area and saw with my own eyes Paula in action. I have to say I walked out as quickly as I walked in. I mean really, what do you do? Ask, do you need help? Did you drop something? Are you looking for something? You just blink your eyes a couple of times, try to figure out what you just saw and who you just saw and then go back to the dry storage area in five minutes when the action is over. *Restaurants should offer a "red light" room.*

I made lots of dressings and salads, sliced fruits and cheeses, which were used to make decorative mirror displays for the buffet lines. I peeled way too many carrots and potatoes. (Look Dan Quayle, I spelt it right!) I was slicing carrots and celery when the executive chef came over with his tape measure and measured my vegetables and said to me, "3 1/2 inches," then told me to fix the sticks that were too long and chop the short sticks for salad, and left. Here I thought I was doing a good job.

Then I was transferred to work in banquets. This is where the psychos work (not that they aren't throughout this business, but this is where they gather.) Talk about high levels of stress, caffeine, drugs and many hours of work. Oh, yeah, and did I say drugs? People want to eat their food at seven o'clock. The food must be ready for seven o'clock, not six-thirty, not seven-thirty but seven o'clock. Six hundred meals needed to go out, so we plugged in the eighteen-foot conveyor belt and began plating. The conveyor belt is placed parallel alongside a large steel table, and each cook would take their place in line. Each cook reaches over the belt to the pans of the meat, potato, vegetable and garnish are placed on the table in front of them. They place the food on the plate as it rolls by. (Think of I Love Lucy and the chocolate episode as the candy moved in front of Lucy and Ethel.) One man puts the plates on the belt, the next adds the potato or starch, the third adds the vegetable, the fourth adds the meat or seafood, the fifth adds the sauce, the sixth adds the garnish and wipes the rims of the plates and the seventh adds the lid and stacks them on the wait staff's tray. By ten minutes of seven, all the plates are done and the wait staff is carrying them out. Everyone is happy. The chef smiles, says, "Good job, men," and we start prepping for the next function. Wait. What? No lunch break? Where's my half hour break? There is no "break" in the food service industry. You eat when you can and where you can. You don't stop. If you stop then everyone stops. This is when the cocaine comes in handy. You need that energy boost to get you through. I don't know a single banquet house where half of the cooks aren't on some substance or another, whether it's liquid, powder or pills. This terrified me.

I had never made an omelet in sauté pan before. In diners you just pour the egg over the flat-top and add the vegetables, cook, fold, it's that simple. I was given one chance to master my omelets skills. *By the way, that's not too many chances.* I got the pan hot, added all the raw vegetables, sautéed them, and then added the eggs. I let the pan do the job of molding the omelet. With a rubber spatula I pulled up on the cooked egg and let the wet portion on top run underneath to continue cooking. This reduces as much juice from the top in order to flip the omelet over. Yes, into the air and back into the pan. Adding the cheese and folding the omelet and placing it on the plate. That was my one chance and I was shoved out into the banquet room on Super bowl Sunday filled with 1,400 people all wanting Sunday morning brunch and omelets.

I was 19 years old and my father had just passed away eight months before this omelet Super bowl Sunday. I clearly remember asking, "Dad, are you proud of me? Send me a sign." A short while later as I was cooking omelets and not looking at the guests a man asked if I would make him an omelet.

I said, "Yes," and looked up at him and he was a priest. *Goosebumps all over my body. I knew this was my sign.*

He said to me, "There are many omelets stations here in this room, but I felt compelled to come over here to you." *Thank you Dad!*

Scared half to death, I managed to work my way out of banquets and into the fine dining kitchen for the last three weeks of my internship. This opened my eyes to more sexual harassment. The male cooks would whistle at the waitresses… or waiters, depending on their preference. There was more nudity, swearing, and lots of sweat. Kitchens can get as hot as 116°. I once saw a cook just whip his pants right off and cook in the buff. What do you do when you see something like that? You whistle Julie Andrew's, "*My favorite things*," pay no attention to the naked guy next to you and do your job.

I came home in April of 1990 and began to work at a southern influenced restaurant called the Carolina House in Kinderhook, NY. I got the job because my mother worked with the owner's sister and Mom said, "My son is coming home and needs a job." The sister talked to the owner, and the rest was history. That's how it is in the food industry. Jobs are given by recommendations, not talent. It's whom you know and when they need you. The right place, the right time. *That seems to be the story of my life. I know I'm not the most talented person in the culinary business, far from it, but I love this business, and that makes up for any loss in talent in my eyes.* At the Carolina House the boss was a complete hot head. He was just like my father. He would scream. He would yell. He was a swearing, ranting lunatic. His whole family worked there with him. The owner made all the desserts and man could he make a great key lime pie. His best though was the Dutch apple crumb. I took notes.

I learned that if the cooks befriend the bartender, the bartender will give you free shots of vodka in your soda.

I learned then mastered the true definition of blackened. And this is also where I got my technique down for breading: one dry hand, one wet hand—don't get the dry hand wet. I breaded lots of chicken for their one thousand spice chicken entrée and plenty of onions for their famous onion ring loaf. We made barbeque sauces, baby back ribs, blackened catfish, Louisiana lemon-pecan trout, corn fritters, beer battered chicken tenders, lots of creoles and jambalaya. I worked through college at the Carolina House.

I graduated college in May of 1992 and took a job with Harry M. Stevens. Now Harry M. Stevens is a concessions company that sought to control all the food contracts of arenas, colleges and stadiums. They were one of the internship programs that brought me to Louisville, Kentucky, to work two

Kentucky Derby's and a Breeder's Cup at Churchill Downs, in 1991 and 1992. What an experience. Mass production of food, banquets all over again. The weak are chewed up and spit out, the desperate get more desperate and the few, like me, conquer it.

I was afraid of banquets in Florida at the resort but I got over that fear working for Harry M. Stevens. I took control. I fought back. I had to learn to be as psycho as the psychos so that I didn't get chewed up, spit out, left crying and shaking in the corner, getting kicked, spit or pissed on. *It's a glamourous life. Trust me. I've seen it and it ain't pretty.* In light of it all, I get as much of a rush from the physical act of getting the work done as the person in the walk-in cooler sniffing their coke. I stay focused, in control, and if a crisis comes along (and they always do), I'm ready for it. Like when the guy beside me (number four on the conveyor belt) overdosed and fell to the floor in the middle of a 436 count meal… I stayed focused. I did his job and mine.

So there I was putting both the meat and the sauce on the plates as they rolled in front of me, and oh yeah, you can't let any of the sauce hit the rim of the plate. The sauce is a delicate job. You need a steady hand and a side towel because the rim of the plate must be clean. More fun came that day because we made a bordelaise sauce with a crème anglaise swirl for the filet mignon. Now the crisis came because I needed to swirl the crème anglaise and drag a toothpick through it to make a web effect in the sauce. 187, 263, 401 and finally 436 comes along. But you don't stop there, because you have to count on the wait staff dropping some to the floor. Or the person who complains, "My food's cold" or "I didn't order chicken," so usually we make twenty extra plates. Meanwhile, Jack Shit is on the ground from his overdose. I'm the one who worked harder and faster and didn't get any more money for doing his job while he was on vacation on the floor. Jack Shit was back at work the next week.

Workers are hard to keep in this industry, and consistency is even harder, so workers are kept even if they're repeat drug users, violent or if they call out often. In food service, you basically need to kill a person to get fired. *Just paroled for attempting to kill your girlfriend? We have a job for you.*

I left Harry M. Stevens and moved back to Albany, NY, in April, 1993. I applied at a lot of restaurants in the Albany area. Got some interviews. Blew some interviews. Turned a lot of work down. Then, as fate would have it, I applied for a job at the Shipyard Restaurant. I guess I fit their profile—young, military looking, well dressed. I was called in on a work trial along with three other chefs and worked for a shift. Long story short, I got the job. This was my only job I ever had that didn't come from a recommendation.

As I said earlier, I liked to run my credit cards up then not pay them *well, kinda still do.* One of them was my car loan. My car was repossessed not once, but twice. *I didn't learn the first time.* The second time it happened Scott and Kathy (the owners of The Shipyard) gave me a loan to get my car back. Scott always said he would remember me as being the only employee to have a car repossessed from his parking lot *twice.*

I worked under a chef who graduated from the CIA (Culinary Arts Institute of America) named Joe. Sometimes

I felt like his little brother, sometimes I felt like his worst enemy.

The Shipyard offered continental cuisine, serving duck, escargot, liver, frog legs, sweetbreads, shark, squid and caviar on its menu.

They were a second family for me. We were all close—too close sometimes—because everybody knew when someone was getting married, fighting, getting divorced and other things too, like your sexual fetishes... that sort of thing. Wicked Wanda, for example... she would come running in the kitchen telling us about the hot man at the bar and in doing so, she would pull her shirt tight to show her hard nipples poking through her blouse. Or there was the waiter who pulled his dick out and slapped the waitress while she was picking something up off the ground. There was a chef who was sleeping with the restaurant manager. The restaurant manager was sleeping with a female server. That, of course, all depended on the week because, as we all knew, she switch hit. I knew which of my fellow workers had infections down below. I knew which infections. I also knew who supplied the coke. Nothing is private in the restaurant field. Nobody feels harassed; it's second nature.

I left the Shipyard for a year when I moved to Connecticut with a partner. I worked at a Sheraton in Waterbury as the Restaurant Chef. I interviewed for either the restaurant chef or banquet manager position. I was given the position of the restaurant chef because it was a lower position and a person named Brian with a great big degree from a grand old culinary college was given the banquet manager position. Big degree, better chef? Nope. Big Degree Brian once sent out 300 undercooked (almost raw) chicken breast dinners. There were many more problems circling Brian like the crows of Troy. His inability to do his job, coupled with inconveniently timed poker rounds on the job made for a bit of a rough time.

My time at the Sheraton was bittersweet. It was a job. I learned menu planning, supervised a staff of 14 people, and was on a 24 hour call when the hotel employees tried to Unionize.

About a year later the hotel filed chapter 11, and my personal relationship went sour. So I left all three—the Sheraton, my relationship, Connecticut—and returned to the Shipyard. I worked there on and off for four years until June of 1997.

Then, I took off to Paris for a holiday. I was there for a short while, but was a kid in a candy store. I was everywhere and eating up as much information as I could before returning home. Although I didn't work there, Paris was an amazing experience. I walked around a lot. I ate at all the corner bistros. I didn't know it then but it proved to be time well spent.

It was in Paris where I hung out with a friend who was studying there. Just before she returned to The States, I visited her. "I don't want to be a tourist," I told her. I wanted to live "la vie" and I wanted to do "faire" the everyday things ordinary people did, like the side street cafés and shoppes that the average tourist overlooks.

My bags stayed at the Hotel Pratic, 9, rue d'Ormesson and we went everywhere in Paris. Mostly we walked because that's what you do. You walk. You walk up and down the Seine, around Notre Dame, the Eiffel Tower, Champs-Elysees, trying this, trying that. We must have hit forty places a day, big and small. I had countless cups of *café au lait*. *Looking back at small little bistros and coffee shoppes, is there any doubt my trip to Paris had any influence with creating Ambition?*

Upon returning from Paris I looked for another job. *Had to pay off those run up credit cards… maybe.* I took up a job here and there but my next real career move was to the College of Saint Rose in Albany, NY. I worked for a company called Aramark. Aramark, like Harry M. Stevens, buys the rights to control all the food contracts of colleges and arenas. It was September of 1997.

My friend Greg Turgeon worked there at the time and, of course, he said, "I can get you in." More proof. It's not what you know, it's whom you know.

I was the evening Location Manager of the Camelot Room. This is the cafeteria where off-campus commuting students would get breakfast, lunch or dinner. I was the guy who would work until midnight, overseeing the registers, babysitting all the help who would much rather hold up a wall than work. After work we were allowed to clean the entire place with a crew… *if* they came in for their shift. If the employee didn't come in, it was just one more thing for me to do. That was my job and I was doing it. I did learn about impulse items and their displays in retail stores. Impulse items are things like candy bars or cookies. Something a guest would grab last minute and create a larger sale. These items usually earn a high profit margin for the store.

So while at Aramark, every now and then the bakery person would call out of work. It was then that I knew I'd be the guy responsible for baking the next day's muffins. "How wonderful, Marc. You have a degree in culinary arts. You can make the muffins while the bakery person is out," said my manager. I didn't get paid for it but the bakery person got her sick time. *Stretch and bend, take it like a pro!*

Two things happened that made me leave One. I told my boss I wanted to see Elton John at the local concert venue. I submitted my request and received confirmation. I bought the tickets. Two days before the show my boss told me I couldn't go because I had no time to use to take the night off. "I have two personal days," I told my boss. "I want to use one of them for this night." (According to Aramark, personal days aren't for personal use. They're for emergencies only: flat tires, broken filling dentist trips, or sick kids. "This is how personal days are rewarded at Aramark," explained their HR rep.)

"Wednesday night I'll have a flat tire." That was that.

Two. I was denied a yearly salary increase. Allegedly, I wasn't effective in a few areas and had some improvements to make. My overall performance didn't seem to meet the high and mighty standards of Aramark. *Maybe because I was the bakery person instead of the manager. Maybe because I was the dishwasher instead of the manager.* Maybe that's why I wasn't effective. As it turned out, Aramark has mystery shoppers who come in and rate an establishment on cleanliness and professionalism: are the name tags appropriately placed, are the uniforms appropriately pressed, are the greetings genuinely greet able? Hey. Hi. Hello. Thank you. You're welcome. I hope you enjoyed your meal. Eye contact. Do come back again. Timely service. Cleanliness of the establishment. Stocked items very neat and orderly.

There are about thirty areas on this review. I received a 100%. I believe I was the only manager that year to receive 100% on a mystery shopper review. Even still, my manager still kept me on a sixty-day review. If I dedicated just a little more to my job (maybe blood, maybe a testicle) and showed the company I was trying harder I would one day get my salary increase.

After all was said and done, the sixty-day review was over and I was told my salary couldn't be adjusted until the next year when the new payroll budget came out. My manager was a young guy and didn't know everything there was to know. In fact, I don't think he knew everything he needed to know to manage breakfast, lunch and dinner in a cafeteria. He admitted to me in my company closing interview (behind closed doors, of course) that he made a mistake. Maybe *he* should have been put on a sixty-day review.

It's New Year's Eve, 1998, and it was Greg who saw my potential as a business owner and chef. He asked if he were to buy a building with a restaurant in it, would I be able to operate it. *Well, since April 10, 2000, Ambition is going strong. I guess the answer was yes! It was this night we started creating Ambition.*

But first, I went to work for Sodexho at SUNY Albany, State University of New York, January of 1999. Like Aramark and Harry M. Stevens, Sodexho vies for food contracts of colleges, arenas and corporations. Drama and chaos. *Nobody* knew what they were doing. So, the SUNY account was just appropriated by Sodexho when I was hired. I took the job of production manager—$33,000. I worked under a man named Patrick who I worked with at Aramark. There are four main quads at SUNY Albany: Dutch, State, Indian and Colonial. Each quad is a twenty-story dorm building housing students. On the bottom floor of each quad is a cafeteria where we worked. I worked at Dutch quad for two months before I was transferred to State.

The man I worked for at State was a short little hot-headed guy. In place of height he used anger. Several times he would call me in after just getting home from a shift just to have me finish work that the dishwashers were supposed to do. I was stupid enough to return. Why? Because I needed that job. And he knew it. Mind games. That sort of thing turned out to be company policy because I got the treatment from this guy *and* corporate. He was the only person who could scream, swear and throw things in the kitchen of a corporation and not suffer any consequences even after oral warnings were issued. They were blind to him. I went over his head a couple times demanding something be done about his behavior. *This only aggravated his piss gland.* Sedexho suggested anger management; the problem was solved… until my car's trunk was kicked in. Big mystery. Then, along comes the transfer. *I still wonder who kicked my trunk in… and why I was transferred to another quad!*

I was furious. I worked hard to get the lowest food cost percentage—the proportion of money used to buy food—of all four quads at the university—28%. All the other quads fell somewhere between 31%-39%. Nevertheless, no good deed goes unpunished. However, with age comes wisdom. If I ever work for someone else again, I'll never tolerate any of the crap I put up with in, all the fear, intimidations, and threats.

This next kitchen I was transferred to, Alumni quad, was undergoing a new training procedure. They were introducing a new food line named Crossroads. I was one of four people chosen to study the new cooking systems and procedures. That took four weeks to learn, but, by this time, I had enough. On opening day of the semester, with 30,000 kids on campus, I handed in my letter of resignation and quit that day. Sodexho was the only job I've ever walked out on and I would do it all over again. It was January 18, 2000. Whenever I hear Marc Anthony singing "*I Need To Know*," that song reminds me of that time. Musical memories, I hold on to good ones and bad ones.

After quitting Sodexho, I decided that it was a good time to be unemployed. I had some savings to live off of and I could see the light that was at the end of the tunnel. Blasting Dolly Parton's song "*9 To 5*" came in handy during these next months. (Just listen to the words. She's an amazingly talented woman. Maybe the words can help you too.) This was when Greg and I got serious about Ambition.

Greg and I then drove down the East Coast from New York to Florida stopping at coffeehouses along the way. We went on a quest, to create a great business. *I like to think we did it.*

We researched demographics and buildings in Kinderhook, Albany and Chatham, all in New York State, but it was Schenectady that Greg wanted to help make a better business neighborhood. We were on Jay Street with the prospect of renting a storefront that formerly housed a florist. When we learned the financial costs of converting a non-restaurant establishment into a restaurant, that deal dead ended.

Feeling discouraged, we walked Jay Street and just four buildings down past the rental we just looked at, my keys fell out of my jacket. How my keys fell out of my jacket is still a mystery but as I bent over to pick them up and as I was coming back up at the same time, both Greg and I saw the Old Jay Tavern with a little *For Sale* sign in its window. This brings me back to a year ago when Greg asked me if he bought a building with a restaurant in it, would I be able to operate it. Now, right in front of us stood a building with a restaurant in it, which was for sale. And how symbolic is it that my keys, of all things, dropped right in front of this building.

The Law of Attraction. We wanted a building. We found a building. *Or maybe it found us.*

CHAPTER 8

So Where's the Pizza? And Other Customer Assumptions

I guess in this day and age it's easy to make assumptions about what a restaurant or retail store is going to be like by the way the storefront appears or by the way the menu reads. Other hints may be flags—literally, flags. The Italian flag for example, it indicates something about the possible presence of Italian food. And what about a life size statue of Betty Boop on roller skates holding a serving tray, what kind of food would one expect?

One customer thought "pizza shop," and asked, "Where's the pizza?"

We looked at him strangely and said, "We don't have pizza."

He stated that he saw Betty Boop. She was outside holding a serving tray. Which led *him* to the assumption that we have pizza.

"Well, maybe if there was a pizza on Betty's tray we might agree with you but, since there's no pizza out there on Betty's tray, there's no pizza in here."

Our name is Ambition Coffee & Eatery, Inc. it is in bold print on the sign hanging outside the building. Can it be any clearer? We have customers who came in and asked, do you guys serve coffee here? There's always the horrible temptation to say no, we don't have coffee here, but if you cross the street and see Beth at that architect office, go upstairs next to the secretary's station, I'm sure that there's a pot brewing. Instead, we just point to the cappuccino machine, the coffee beans, and then the other coffee products. So to anyone else who is wondering, absolutely, we serve coffee.

I finished with those customers who didn't know we were a coffee house. Then, as I was standing behind the bar playing with the CD player, a man came in and sat on a stool behind me at the bar. Before I was able to say anything he opens up his mouth and asks, "What's in the back room?"

"A lounge for customers to sit with coffee, read the paper, a magazine, maybe just relax."

"Why would I want to do that?" he replied.

"Well," I conjured, "I think we're just offering ambience."

"Well that's stupid."

"You're right. It's Stupid!

At the same time, another man was drinking his coffee, and a CD called "*Music from the Coffee lands*", was playing. He said to me, "Are you changing the music soon?"

The CD has Brazilian singers with guitars and some low-key drum beats. Calm, relaxing, and just over-all mellow. I wasn't too sure what he was referring to but thought the age old "no" would suffice. So I didn't even stop what I was doing and was still sifting through CD's with my back to him trying to find George Michael's CD "*Listen Without Prejudice*" but then my curiosity got the better of me. "Why?"

"Because it sucks!"

"Alrighty than Mr. Santana, I'll take your musical opinion into consideration," I said to him. I should have noticed what I was doing. I had my hands on all these CD's, shuffling through them looking for George Michael's CD, "*Listen Without Prejudice.*" Again, could it have been anymore clear? Listen… without…prejudice…

Just listen to those men complain. Like water off a ducks back. Nope, not me. I let it bother me. I let them get the best of me and my ego just ate it right up. They pissed me right off!

So instead of taking it to the next level, which probably would've consisted of more nine-year-old boy back-and-fourth banter, I opted to step outside, get some fresh air, and just take a walk. I walked out of the restaurant ranting to myself. I was no sooner outside when I heard the sound of a cart being pushed. Then I heard the sounds of glass bottles clinking together. As I approached the side alley off of Jay Street to continue my walk I ran right into that homeless man I saw pushing his shopping cart up Union Street. We practically collided.

"Sorry brother," his voice is deep with a southern accent, his bright white eyes, a big smile and white teeth.

I couldn't help but smile back at him.

Then he started to laugh and said, "Yeah, I'm just trying to clean up the neighborhood. Ya gotta do yer part, gotta do yer part."

This made me smile even more and I asked him if he wanted any more bottles. "Oh, I'll take as many as I can get," he said. "I use the money to buy me some food at the City Mission and what's ever left over I give to Father Rogers over at the church." I told him I have bottles for him not mentioning how many I have. We enter the restaurant. He was going to leave the shopping cart outside but I told him he better bring it in. "No, it ain't right to bring my cart in here. I can walk the bottles out." Then I showed him the 15 cases of bottles and his eyes popped out and his jaw dropped like he just won the lottery. And there was that smile again and a tear ran down his cheek. He walked two cases out at a time until they were all gone and couldn't say enough of how grateful he was and what he was going do with the money.

I shook his hand and said, "I'm Marc."

He said, "I'm Freddie, but friends call me Kirby. You can call me Kirby."

"Well, Kirby," I said, "it was nice to meet you and you come back again for more bottles."

"Oh, I will, I will, yes, sir-re, I'll be back. Have a good day now, brother, and God bless ya." As he was about to leave he turned around and said to me, "Oh, brother, here's a feather for you. I pick them up; it's my way of knowing the big guy upstairs is looking after me. I hope you enjoy it." He walked out and I felt so good. I had completely forgotten the reason I left the restaurant in the first place and when I saw those two men still sitting at the bar and I remembered why I left, none of it mattered anymore. Divine intervention. *Who gave me that idea to take a walk?* Kirby you're my "*Jolly Mon Sing*," thanks Jimmy Buffet.

Ambition is on a pedestrian walkway, so there's foot traffic; people walking around, shopping, strolling, whatever. I can understand going into a pottery store or bookstore and looking around. But to walk into a restaurant and just look around, why does a person do this? Okay, maybe if you're going to do this, at least read the menu; take a take-out menu or a business card maybe? Why did you enter a restaurant in the first place? For information. (I'm assuming.) Would you be coming back at a later time? Why do people walk in, look around, then leave? Does this happen at other restaurants that I'm not aware of? I've never walked through a restaurant and then left. I'm going to walk right in, right through, and right out of Tavern On The Green in New York City one of these days; let's see how that flies. *Or maybe I should say lets see how I fly as I'm thrown out.*

This is a little hurray to everyone in the business who's working because they have rent to pay or a mortgage, maybe a school loan, (acting and singing lessons aren't free either). You're greeting a table, telling them the beverage specials, food specials, bringing them their food, refilling their beverages, checking up, asking how their meals are, coming back to ask if they want dessert, then reciting the desserts... only to have them decline. You clear their plates and glasses, pick up the dirty silverware and napkins (yes that napkin, the one they blew their nose in) add their check twice, (the first time they didn't give you their coupon), and finish by cleaning the table. After the guest leaves you discover a mass card from the local church was left as your gratuity. *Maybe the bank will accept this card as fifteen more dollars in my deposit?*

Why do people call us at looking for the name and phone number of another restaurant on the street? Do they really think I'm going to give that information out? I want their business. They called Ambition because of the hard work and money we spent on advertising. Now I'm supposed to just give that other restaurant free advertising and business by passing along information? Let them work as hard as we did getting their name out there. By calling us asking about another restaurant's name or phone number on the street, who is my competitor, what am I supposed to say, "Would you like me to call for you and make reservations?"

A woman ordered our house salad and upon receiving it, she looks at it and said, "What is this?"

"What is what?" replies Maria.

The woman then replied, "This lettuce. What is it?"

Maria holds her laugh in and said, "Its mesclun mix. It's a mixture of baby greens."

"Oh," she said, "I've never seen this before."

Welcome to the new millennium.

I had dumped whole coffee beans in a coffee cup to transfer them when a customer saw me with the cup and said, "Really good coffee. A little bit crunchy, but good."

A woman sat in the restaurant and ordered a burger. Stacy's personality is a cross between Joan Jett and Anne Murray.

She's totally a rocker but she has that sweet maternal side to her. This particular day she's Anne Murray. So Stacy asked her, "How do you want your burger cooked?"

This woman's response was, "What do you mean, how do I want my burger cooked? I want it cooked. I don't want no blood!"

This woman calls Stacy over again and said, "There's something wrong with the iced tea."

Stacy's answer is, "It's unsweetened."

"Well, I don't like it," she said.

Stacy then asked, "What would you like to drink?"

"Give me a soda," the woman said.

"What kind of soda?" Stacy asked. Part of waiting tables is extracting information out of the guests so they get exactly what they want. (This decreases waste but can by as painful as pulling a tooth... for both parties. Isn't it a common practice to know what kind of soda you like? I know I like Coke. I'm not going to say, give me a soda. I'm going to say, "Give me a Coke.")

"I don't care," the woman responded.

"Coke?" Stacy answered.

"No, not Coke. I can't have caffeine." (icing tea, this lady apparently thinks, takes out the caffeine.) "Get me a Sprite," she says, quite annoyed.

I was just relieved that Stacy was Anne Murray and not Joan Jett that day.

We often work understaffed at Ambition because we would all rather be a little busier than work with some lazy, dumbass, no common sense, waste of a mind and payroll. A normal morning for me is preparing soups, slicing meats and cheeses, preparing my produce, pounding burgers, making tuna salad, rotating inventory, answering the phone, taking take-out orders, chit-chatting with guests, pouring coffees, making cappuccinos, running the register, cooking the food orders, clearing tables, and washing dishes. *Is all that even was a sentence? My editor's gonna love that one!*

One particular morning was overly busy. It would be easy to say that things were going a little crazy. Now on top of everything else I was doing, I took a table—probably wasn't a smart choice for me but I really didn't have too much of a choice, a father and his daughter. I brought them menus and asked which beverages they'd like. They said they were ready to order.

"Okay," I said, "What would you like?" Rolling my pad over to a clear page and clicked open my pen.

The daughter said, "I want over-medium eggs, not runny, but not well done."

Not too sure how to respond, I said, "So you want your eggs over-medium-well?"

She said, "I don't want them soft and gushy, and I don't want them hard cooked."

I'm starting to lose my patience now. I'm thinking of all the 10 things I do need to be doing right now on top of waiting on this table. I strain my eyes and turn my head in a not-so-sure-of-what-she-wants sort of way, and once again I said, "So you want your eggs over-medium-well, correct?"

Thankfully, she agreed. I then ask her another tough question, "What kind of toast would you like?"

"What kind of toast do you have?"

My patience now just ran out. I hear the phone ringing but Maria is with a guest and I'm with this woman who can't decide what kind of toast she likes, and the phone is now on its fourth ring, so I said, "Today for toast we have purple peas and poppy seeds." Very calmly like every restaurant offers this flavor.

She didn't know how to respond to that, so she then piped in with, "Do you have rye toast?"

"Yes," I said, "we have rye. Would you like that instead of the purple peas and poppy seeds?" Now I laugh.

As I'm laughing, she too is laughing and said to me, "You don't really have purple peas and poppy seeds toast, do you?"

"No, but it does sound delicious doesn't it?"

After laughing, that seemed to bring everything back into perspective. The phone was answered, the wave of traffic seemed to stop for a while and we were able to get organized enough to pull ourselves "out of the weeds."

Some restaurant owners don't like other restaurants (or restaurant owners) in the same area—namely, me. Maybe it's a pride thing, ego or competition. It's probably a lot of things. When a new restaurant is coming into town, I want to know all the information about the place. Basically, I want to know how it's going to effect my bottom line.

John, who works at the post office and is a good customer, came in and told me about this new restaurant opening soon.

I asked all the questions I wanted answered about the atmosphere and his response to me was, "No place will ever rival Ambition. This place is just gushing with ambience," he said with his loud jovial laugh.

I later told John his little comment made my book and soon the world would know who he is. John's response was, "The world isn't ready," laughing out loud again. High-five to you John.

Imitation is the most sincere form of flattery, or so I was told. In this business, I really need to be aware of competition, especially if they're targeting… my customers.

A restaurant opened up here on Jay Street. I won't mention the name because it's not worth mentioning. Here's my reasoning. While writing and developing a business plan, this new business owner ate at Ambition all that spring and summer. This businessperson then submitted the business plan to Schenectady Economic Development Corporation (SEDC) for a low interest loan. Soon after, Greg and I were asked by SEDC if we had a business interest in this new restaurant that was soon to be opening. Surprised by the question and curious we said, "No, why?"

SEDC told us, they used your name, Ambition, as a reference. They said if they took 20% of your business it would keep their doors open, and they counted the number of people who walked in, what they ate and how much money it would have generated. Then, to boot, this owner asked my staff business questions about where we buy our coffee and other related questions. Now I ask you to put yourself in my shoes. How would you react if this person's sole focus was targeting a business plan at your customers, would you like this new business? I'm not sure what you would do but I'm putting my boxing gloves on and I'm entering the ring. I'm not leaving until one of us is down! How about some Elton John, *"I'm Still Standing."*

Okay, you people on cell phones. Put yourself in our position. We're trying to take your order, and you're talking to someone else on the phone. This is a bad combination. It never mixes well. You inevitably miss something when juggling... but to make up for it you blame us for screwing up. Put the cell phone away and order. The same goes for the loud speaker conference call. People throughout the restaurant do not want to hear your conversations. Shut it off. Better yet, inconvenience yourself not the people around you, and go outside. *I just want to take those cell phones and drop them in the sink.*

Parents and babies, I don't understand how a grown adult takes a child/infant to a restaurant, feeds the child, and in the process makes such a mess with the food, (mostly Cheerios... and Cheerios get everywhere. (By the end of the day we find the Cheerios ten tables away). Left behind are bibs, pacifiers, stuffed animals, bottles, plastic keys and sippy cups all left for us to clean up. *Don't you want all your things back?* Do these parents practice this at home? Who cleans up after them? *We're servers, not maids.*

The show *Thoroughly Modern Millie* just finished running at Proctor's and a cast member came in the restaurant for a snack before he took off for the next town. He pointed at an apple square and all I heard was, "apple square." So my first reaction is to tell him the price. We are in Schenectady and that's everyone's first question, how much does it cost?

I said, "$1.50 plus tax."

The cast member then said to me, "I didn't ask the price. I asked if it was an apple square."

Embarrassed, I offered him my apology and explained how I didn't listen to his question, but I assumed the answer because I so often hear, "How much does that cost?" I then said to him, "Yes, in fact it is an apple square." *That's what happens when I assume!*

CHAPTER 9

The Customer Is Always Right. Maybe I Should Be a Little More Flexible.

I've learned over the years that not everyone is Ambition's customer. This was a hard pill to swallow because at one time I did try to please everyone in my restaurant. But I've learned that even by beating myself up emotionally, I can't please every guest.

There are just some folks who want a four dollar lunch and aren't going to pay any more, period.

Then there are the folks who enjoy being miserable. We all know them. I'm sure you can name someone in your life who enjoys being miserable. They'll always look for the worst and expect it. And no matter how many cartwheels, summersaults, and back flips my staff and I do, still, it won't be enough to make a guest happy. If being miserable is what the guest wants when he or she walks through our door, that's what they'll be.

Third, we don't offer chicken nuggets, french fries, fried mozzarella sticks or pizza. If that's something your child wants, take that child where they serve those foods; don't be angry with us because we don't offer them.

When these problems come up, and they do, I just take a deep breath and do my best. And that is all I can do.

I was approached by a man who was filming an independent movie on Jay Street; he asked if he could shoot a scene in the restaurant.

He described the scene and said to me, "It's a minute and a half, but will probably take about half an hour to forty-five minutes to shoot." I agreed. He asked me if I wanted to read the script and I declined. I informed him that we were going to have a busy day, and the only opportunity he would have is to come in at three p.m. before our dinner rush. He agreed. We also spoke of other things, namely the CD player. I asked him, "I hope the CD player isn't going to have to be shut off?"

He responds, "No."

So the next week, they came in, started setting up and asked me questions about where they could stand and shoot scenes. I gave them some suggestions depending on where the high traffic areas for the wait staff were going to be. I should have known five minutes into it that this was a bad idea. Almost two hours later they were still in the restaurant, still filming and still in everyone's way. The employees were tripping over wires and bumping into the crew people, guests couldn't get their take out orders because there were twelve crew members hovering around the bar, and customers were uncomfortable being in this movie.

Ambition isn't a big place. The camera guy was moving the camera everywhere it was least convenient, the director was yelling, "Cut" or "Do over" or some such thing every two minutes, the lights guy was blinding the customers, the actors in Mexican uniforms with huge sombreros provided a carnival atmosphere which wasn't in keeping with our décor. By the third scene they were filming, there was a male actor in a dress sitting at one of the tables. Not a pretty man, I might add; full beard, hairy legs and work boots, but in a pretty blue dress.

An actress at my bar was stealing chocolate-covered espresso beans. I caught her putting the lid back on the container and eating the beans then she said to me, "I may as well buy two danishes; I can't just sit here and not buy something!"

Thoughtful of you, but I wish you had just paid for the espresso beans that you stole and ate!

Now the director approached and asked me to shut off the CD player because it was causing too much noise in the background.

That's when I lost it. *Cancer the Crab, SNAP!* Don't mess with my music! I walked over to the producer who originally asked me to do the shoot in the restaurant and I said to him, "You and your crew will be out at 5pm," which was in fifteen minutes. And then I walked away. Breathe, I said to myself.

His director or whoever this fellow was walked over to me and said, "We need a little more time to finish the shoot, but in order for us to finish the shoot, you need to be a little more flexible, if you want us to film our movie in your restaurant. If you're not going to flexible, we're going to take our movie to another restaurant on the street."

I looked him dead in the eye and said, "Exactly how fast can you be out?"

Then to put the icing on the cake, they wrote and delivered a letter to my business partner Greg saying how uninviting I was, and how I kicked them out before their shoot was over. They went on to say that they intended to let everyone know how uncooperative I was and that the only way to get them to keep their comments to themselves was to apologize to them and let them finish the shoot.

I don't respond well to blackmail, especially if I have nothing to lose. This man was the one who had lied to me about the half hour filming. He had lied to me about the filming of only one scene when it was three scenes that they filmed. He was the one, whose actor was stealing the espresso beans, and he was the one who created the chaos in my restaurant, yet he was the one who wanted me to apologize, and be a little more flexible. *Sorry, dude, but my stretch and bend days are over.*

This man came back in a year later. Ate lunch and came to the kitchen and said, "Remember me? I tried to stay away, but your sandwiches are just too good." He smiled and walked away. I'm not sure if he ever came back in after that. *I guess that was his apology.*

Lobster is quite expensive. I believe we've all paid for lobster at one time or another over the years and have come to expect if you want anything with lobster, you're going to pay more for it.

We served lobster raviolis one evening, offering twelve raviolis in this dish. It was accompanied with a roasted garlic, red pepper coulis, side-salad and bread. We charged $17.95 for the meal. We served it that evening and all the guests enjoyed it… except for one. This one particular woman felt she was over-charged for the meal. The portions, she alleged, were too small. She also informed us that she was able to get the same meal at a restaurant in Albany—twenty miles away—for two dollars less. And quite frankly the woman said, "The lobster raviolis were "okay" at best."

I've learned to accept criticism with a grain of salt.

Welcome Linda! What a pleasure it is to have you here today. We're so happy you picked Ambition to be your next horrible dining experience. Linda broke her leg and was uncomfortable with her cast. She automatically took her frustration out on Ambition. First, she picked a booth (ding! Her first stupid mistake) and tried to slide herself in, hitting her leg against the booth and the stand that holds the table up. The scream of agony that was released scared the entire restaurant into complete silence. Of course, her hitting her leg is my fault. Linda decided she couldn't sit in a booth so she moved herself out, hitting her leg again. Another scream and my fault again. She now sat at a table and put her broken leg in the aisle way. (Yep, stupid mistake number two)

A customer came in talking to her friend and not paying attention to where she was walking. Yes, the customer hit Linda's leg. The scream she let out this time... I've only ever heard a mother in labor cry out like this.

Now, Linda was beyond miserable and she received her sandwich. She ordered a New Yorker—grilled roast beef, provolone, onions, mushrooms, horseradish Dijon on sour dough bread. Linda took the time to open her sandwich and count her mushrooms. She only finds three. She sent the sandwich back to the kitchen. At this point, Linda didn't want to talk to the manager (me) and didn't want to pay for her sandwich because of the "three mushrooms," the fact that she was pissed her leg "got beat up" (her words), so she decided to just sit there and watch the rest of the people around her at the table eat. I knew all too well it wasn't going to end there; they still have to give out the Oscar for best actress.

Now the reason Linda came to Ambition in the first place was because she's hungry. Guess what, she's still hungry. But there was nothing at Ambition she would eat. So she now had to leave.

On her way out, leaving all her friends/family behind (because they were all happy), she turned to the wait staff and said what a horrible experience she had at Ambition. She declared that she would never come back, never recommend anyone to visit, and that our sandwiches were over-priced. Out the door she went. The entire restaurant gave a communal sigh as the door closed and she disappeared.

Customers sometimes write me complaining about the experience they had at Ambition. If I feel that the customer is right, I'll send a gift certificate to visit us again. Because that's the reason they're taking the time to write in the first place; they want compensation. The latest letter I received was from guests who visited us while *Spamalot* was playing at Proctor's. The letter stated they had dined with us before and that they enjoyed their meals, even if they were small and didn't fill them. It went on to read that they enjoyed the All-American Cheeseburger we offer—eight ounces of fresh ground black angus beef, sharp cheddar, lettuce, tomato, grilled onions, ketchup, fresh bakery hard roll, homemade potato salad, pickle and a homemade cup of soup. But they said for all the freshness it wasn't worth the money because they still left hungry. Then they went on to write that they've told other people of their experience at Ambition and not to ever go.

About four weeks after receiving this letter a woman came to my kitchen door in the restaurant and said she was a friend of so and so, (click, the light went on) the person who wrote the letter. She told me not to pay attention to the letter. The author of the letter is just a constant complainer and is always looking for something for free. This visitor acknowledged the fact that we do offer great food with healthy portions and she wanted me to know that we were doing a great job. *Thank you!*

Now we have the guest who doesn't know the difference between being sociable from being self-absorbed and annoying.

A man came in every morning for the longest time because he didn't have a job (which is what he told us). He would read the newspaper or library book out loud to my employees as they were working, as if they were just going to stop doing their jobs and listen to him read his stories. Well we did at first, because we do offer customer service. This customer feels we don't need to worry about the other customers: he's here now, and that's all that matters.

After a few weeks of this the staff and I became good at just walking away from him as he was reading his stories to us. This didn't stop him. He just continued to read into thin air. We'd keep walking and he'd keep talking a little louder the farther we got from him. We're a restaurant, not an "open mic."

He did finally get the hint… or maybe he just got a job. But whatever his situation was, he's not reading to us anymore and that is all that matters.

A woman came into the restaurant and ordered a Caesar salad. Then she returned it to me saying, "I could make a better one at home."

That's it? That's your excuse? That's why you're not going to purchase the Caesar salad you just ordered? The same salad that I just paid for ingredients and paid a cook to make for you? That salad that I now have to toss into the trash and declare a food lose because you can make a better one at home? I'm usually understanding of complaints but this particular case was a bitter pill. We make great food here at Ambition so when I hear a statement like, "I can make a better one at home." you'll have to prove it to me.

Here is when I step away from being the owner and step into being a guest. If and when I go out to eat at a restaurant, diner, pub, whatever it is, I want to make sure it's as good as I can make at home. Why pay some restaurant for the food that is prepared by cooks who can't do their job. I completely understand this because it does happen and it has happened to me. Greg hates it when I do this.

He'll say, "Just eat the food!"

No, I'm not going to just eat the twenty-eight dollar New York Sirloin that is medium well when I ordered it medium rare.

So I went out to the table with the Caesar salad in hand and said to the woman, "How can you make this better at home?"

"I would use more croutons," she replied.

"You would use more croutons? How many croutons would you put on this salad to make it better?"

Adamantly she said, "Fifteen."

I took her fork and pulled out the croutons, one by one, counting as I went. At fourteen I stopped. I looked at her and asked, "Shall I continue?"

"...I didn't think there were that many croutons in there."

But the customer is always right.

Oh, the United States and its fine citizens. These fine citizens need to stand in line at unemployment just to be given a piece of paper to be filled out by employers like me to prove to the state that this person is actively looking for work.

This woman got her form from the unemployment office, which is right around the block. She proceeded to walk down Jay Street and entered every store asking if she can have an application. Now, New York State doesn't care if she actually has the skills necessary to work at the places where she's asking for applications, nor does New York State care if she makes an attempt to look presentable or even interested. The State doesn't care. Just walk in, in your dirty jeans, your oversized sweatshirt, greasy hair, untied oversized dragging shoes: "Can I have an application?"

Did you just roll out of bed? Maybe that should be one of the questions on this form New State offers. Prove to us, the State of New York, that you didn't just roll out of bed.

Now, if the employer isn't hiring, this woman will ask the employer to sign a piece of paper that proves she, a fine, upstanding citizen, is actively looking for work and that I, the employer, have no employment for her at this time. So I'm supposed to just sign my name and get her back to her trick or treating.

This woman is obviously overqualified to work at a bookstore, a restaurant, and an architect firm, (two actually) a clothing store, a folklore society, a pottery store, hair salon, cigar shop and Fountain's Inc, an office where they produce maps of geography. *What a talented woman and a fine catch for any of the businesses on Jay Street.*

I refuse to sign. And I refuse to pass out an application. When I refused to sign or give her an application she turns around and tells me, "You have to give me an application. It's against the law for you not to give me an application!"

"We're not hiring and I don't have to give you an application; it isn't against the law."

She proceeded to tell me her mother works for unemployment and that her mother told her that it was against the law for businesses not to give her an application.

"I'm not giving you an application and I'm not signing that piece of paper. You are not actively seeking work."

"Better yet," I said to her. "Make me a cappuccino!"

She was unable to perform to duty.

"What's the difference between a latte and a cappuccino?"

Again, she failed.

Finally, I gave her an easy one, "What side of the guest does the fork belong on?"

She looked at me like I had two heads, and mumbled some answer under her breath, when finally this woman's fine outstanding friend that came along with her on this employment quest said, "Come on, and let's go. He's a scumbag!"

Oh, I see, I'm the scumbag! Thanks for clearing things up for me.

What about the customers who have a little too much to drink before they come to Ambition? To a bartender, this is a nightmare. First, you can't serve them, period. There's too much liability these days. It's my fault you wrapped your car around the telephone pole. How that ever got passed is still beyond me. Nothing like pointing the finger and passing the buck. I'm an alcoholic, I can't stop drinking. It's your fault I'm drunk!

Now, of course we refuse to serve them and all hell breaks loose. We're now in the movie *The Exorcist* with Linda Blair as her head spins and she spews vomit.

"Just give me a fuckin' beer you dumb fucking cunt!"

"*SWM—charming, witty, great sense of humor, likes walks on the beach, seeking DFC.*" A fine catch to bring home to Mom and Dad. *Would you like a drink?*

It was Veteran's Day. Two women came in and ordered their lunch at the counter where the sign hangs, *"Place Take Out Orders Here."*

Sensing there might be something askew, Stacy asks, "That's to go, correct?" (Mind you, Stacy is in her Joan Jett mood, *oh boy.*)

"No," the woman responded, "We'll be eating here."

"Okay. Fine," Stacy thought. Instead of seating them she made them pay for their food first. She was in a feisty mood and they didn't pay mind to read the signs "please seat yourself at any clean table" or "Place Take Out Orders Here."

"You can have a seat, and we'll come over with napkins and your drinks," Stacy said.

They sat down, but ordered a well-done burger and the special of the day (a meatloaf served open-faced over sourdough bread with a tomato sauce, sautéed onions, melted provolone cheese and baked French fries. Apparently, she didn't like the way we prepared the special. We could tell because she said, "I don't want it with all the crap on it. I just want the meatloaf and fries." Well, alrighty then.

Now, when a hamburger comes out of the cooler, it's approximately 38°. To bring it up to a well-done temperature of 160° takes some time. If we were a fast food chain that served two-ounce burgers, that would be pretty easy, but our burgers are eight ounces, hand-shaped, fresh Black Angus ground beef. Twelve minutes later her burger was done, but she's up at the register. "I have to go. I had no idea it would take this long. I've been here for forty minutes. I want my money back!" She went on complaining a little more. She was being so rude that I stepped out of the kitchen to refund the sale and get rid of her. "Nobody is going to come in here and verbally abuse my wait staff. I'm giving you your money back and you can leave."

The woman noticed her food was ready, sitting there on the counter so she said, "I'll eat it here."

"No, that's ok. I'm giving you your money back and you can leave." While refunding the sale I was frazzled, we're busy, twelve tickets were hanging in the kitchen, Godzilla in front of me and my jumpy fingers, so I let Stacy finish refunding the sale so I could get back in the kitchen.

Stacy, *Joan Jett*, said to the lady, "Have a nice day."

"Shut the fuck up!" shouted the women on her way out. Stacy says that woman was her ray of sunshine.

Gratuity, it speaks for itself. If somebody offers you a service, you offer them a monetary reward to thank them. We're all familiar with this practice. We call it "tips" (**T**o **I**nsure **P**roper **S**ervice). We in the food industry are the worst or the best when it comes to tipping. We either tip really well or we tip really bad. But when we don't tip at all it's because the server didn't work for it. We can differentiate between the slow and lazy server and the getting-your-ass-kicked-with-too-much-work server. I lead by example and know, first hand, my servers are usually the latter.

Two men came in, sat down, and ordered two coffees and two breakfast sandwiches. The bill came to ten dollars without tax. Now it should be known that you tip 15-18% minimum on the total *food* bill, not the total food bill *and* tax. With 8% sales tax in New York State, it comes to $10.80.

Those men left a $.60 tip. That's what... 6% maybe? Thanks for the tip. I know we gave them good service. I know they enjoyed their breakfast. So why $.60? Maybe they're just ignorant.

A couple came in for breakfast. It was their second time in. Jeremy said to me, "They were in last week and didn't tip me."

So I said, "Well, see how it goes. Maybe they just forgot."

Jeremy brought them menus, and they ordered two large orange juice, two omelets, French toast, and a blueberry muffin. Everything went well, they enjoyed their food, and they got their bill. The total with tax is $20.79. The man came up to the register and paid the bill. He went back to his seat and talked a little while longer and got up to leave.

Jeremy then walked up to them and said, "Do you need change for a tip?"

"No."

Jeremy said, "So you're not gonna leave a tip? This is your second time in, and you didn't leave me a tip your first time either."

"Really?" the man replied, acting all surprised. He then said, "I thought you didn't have to leave a tip if you went up to the register and paid yourself."

Jeremy said, "No, I provided you with a service by waiting on your table and it is a common practice to leave a tip for the wait staff, regardless if you paid your check yourself at the register."

The man then got to the truth of the matter and said, "You don't got to squeeze me for my money," and he and his friend got up and left.

Reservations. We all want a table in a restaurant at 6:30 on a Friday night so we call for reservations. "Great, Mr. Brown, we'll see you at 6:30. Thanks for calling." Well, Mr. Brown's party showed up at 7:10. 7:10, that's just like 6:30, only later.

If you're running late or not coming, why don't you just call and let us know. Do we need to get out our crystal ball and see where you are or if you're still coming? Do you think we won't notice you didn't arrive? We have a completely full restaurant except one table. Nope we didn't notice you never showed up. Not only did we lose your business, but we lost the revenue that table would have brought us had we been able to give it to someone else. If we had only known your party wasn't going to dine with us that evening. Thank you oh so very much!

In New York State, with the exception of Seeing Eye Dogs, animals are not allowed in restaurants. Most people don't like human hairs in their food, so it stands to reason that they don't want cat or dog hairs floating around and settling on top of their cappuccino either. How about a parrot that flies around and shits on the table? Delicious! What else does your restaurant do for guest entertainment? So why do people with animals continually try to bring them in and just expect it to be okay?

A woman once came with a bird on her shoulder. I looked at the bird, and its head was moving.

I asked the woman, "Is that a real bird on your shoulder?" She said, "No."

Now I'm not an idiot, and I've been to the zoo. This isn't some plastic parrot bobbing on her shoulder like some "B" movie prop. Clearly it was alive. She smiled. I tell her animals aren't allowed in restaurants.

"So I guess I can't get a cup of coffee to go?" she said.

I said, "No, you can't. Not with a live bird on your shoulder."

She left, sighing and annoyed of course. I let out some frustration and I went upstairs. Seconds later, she came back without the bird. Indicating towards me she said to Jeremy, "He's an asshole." She bought her coffee and left. I guess she felt she needed to leave a statement of conviction to prove she was right. I'm the asshole. I'm the bad guy left holding the bag for New York State's Health Department of rules and guidelines and every time customers disagree, probably because it's inconvenient for them at the time. I'm the asshole. Talk about accepting responsibility for your own actions.

A woman who's a regular came in and said that her brother was arrested the night before for robbing two gas stations. She showed me the picture of the man in the paper and said, "Do you recognize him?"

"No, I don't," I responded.

She said, "I just brought him in here last week."

"Oh, really," I said.

She said, "He's only been out of jail for two weeks."

I said, "Well, don't bring him back in here."

"Don't worry," she said. "He's going away for a long time this time."

"I would hope so," I replied. *Is there anybody else you want us to meet? Say like... Ted Bundy, maybe? How about Hannibal Lector?*

A man was eating lunch with his friends at a table, and he got a bloody nose. It happens. I know that if it happened to me I'd probably be a little embarrassed and if it didn't stop soon I'd go to the bathroom until it did. Usually they stop in a minute or two. This man felt nothing wrong with just sitting there using napkin after napkin collecting his blood, missing some in the process and letting it drip on himself, the table and the floor. His nosebleed finally stopped, and there were six to eight bunched up bloody napkins on the table. Yuck. Disgusting. Vile. Gross. They all fit here, just pick your word.

His friend/girlfriend started to clean up his bloody mess, and he stopped her. "The waiter will do it," he said. They left the table, they left the restaurant, and they left the bloody mess. *Did I mention how glamorous the restaurant business is?*

Restroom. We all need to use the restroom. It's a natural bodily function. I understand that. But what I don't understand are the people who come into the restaurant without ordering and expect to use the rest room like it's there for them. We're a restaurant, not a public toilet. It's for the convenience of our paying guests. Do you walk into a neighbor's house and use their bathroom? Wouldn't you at least ask to use the rest room? May I please? Or can I please? Nope. Not here in Schenectady.

My business doors aren't open for people to come right in and use the toilet. Never mind that I pay for the toilet paper, the hand towels, the hand soap, the electricity when they turn on the light switch, the water bill when they flush and wash their hands. Then on top of all that, I get to clean the rest rooms at the end of the day. Hurray! This is one of my favorite jobs. *Yes, this is why I own a restaurant, so I can clean the restrooms.*

We can pick out bathroom runners at Ambition. We've gotten good at it over the years. There are two types. The first one is the fast walker. The fast walker bee-lines for the toilets hoping nobody is going to stop them. The second type simply doesn't make eye contact but looks around for the sign for the restrooms. Since our rest rooms are kind of hidden, usually people need to ask where they are.

In came Mr. Fast Walker one day making a bee-line for the toilet. I've trained my staff to provide customer service. They know to stop a guest at the register, ask, "How are you?" and "How can I help you?" Usually, the person will say he or she needs the bathroom. Then we gently remind them that our bathrooms are for customers only. But if you'd like to buy a cup of coffee or a soda, that's considered being a customer, and we would be honored to have you urinate in our bathroom.

Now I ask you, who walks around a downtown or anywhere for that matter without money? I don't. It doesn't have to be a week's paycheck, but a few dollars... even a five. What mature adult doesn't have sufficient money to buy a cup of coffee? If you have no money then you probably haven't bought anything to drink earlier in the day. Why would such a person always have to pee? And why does it have to be my restaurant? This is one of life's great mysteries. So when the person who doesn't ever have any money enters my restaurant to use the restroom, for some reason they'll became angered when we say, you can't use our facilities. Usually making a scene in the restaurant is the recourse of such people. We become the scum of the earth. Language that would make a sailor blush can be heard coming from these people. "You're fuckin' kidding me! This is fuckin' ridiculous! I'm never fuckin' coming back and I'm telling all my friends." (Oh, if only this one was true! Please tell your friends not to urinate at Ambition.) How many times can you fit the F-word into one sentence? There must be some kind of contest around that I'm not aware of.

A man who is usually a morning customer came in one day, bought nothing, used the restroom and left. I let him go because he comes in every morning for coffee.

About a half hour later another customer came to me and communicated that the bathroom was disgusting. His exact words are unnecessary to repeat here, but the mess was amazing. The morning customer had lost control of his bowels in the bathroom. Adding insult to injury, he left his dirty underpants behind the toilet bowl. I assumed he thought nobody would notice them. *This is the elegant side of diners. Maybe he thought we were the dry cleaners?*

Another guy walked in really fast one day heading for the bathroom. Once again, we put the "Can we help you?" brakes on him.

"I need to use the bathroom," he replied.

"You need to be a customer," we reminded him.

"I'll buy a cup of tea," he said.

So everything appeared to be fine. Well, he was gone for about ten minutes, his tea cooled to room temperature, when he finally came out. He sipped his tea. Meanwhile, someone else went and used the rest room. The new customer came back holding his nose and said, "WOW!"

The tea-sipping man said, "I really had to go."

The man holding his nose said, "I saw!"

So the man sipping his tea went back into the restroom again. An odor started to fill the restaurant. The tea-sipping man came back out of the restroom, immediately paid for his tea and left. Once again, we all looked at each other. Who'll be the brave one to see what kind of a mess we have on our hands this time? Yes, it was another massacre. At least this time the charming man tried to clean up after himself, which is why he went back in the second time. His work was inadequate. Fecal matter was smeared all over the floor and toilet bowl. *Somebody pinch me and wake me from this wonderful dream.*

A woman entered Ambition with a Stewart's coffee cup. (Stewart's is a local convenience store.) She also had a bag from CVS with goodies in it. She wanted to use my bathroom. She brought her cup of coffee from Stewart's, she shopped at CVS and now she wants to use my bathroom? *Just give her a black eye and be done with it.*

So far, the women's room seems to have gotten away unscathed. Not so. Ladies, don't go thinking you're all angels because you're not.

A woman came over to me one day and whispered, "I think I made a mess in the ladies' room."

"Okay, thanks for telling me. I'll clean it up." And what a mess it was. Her monthly visitor. Understandable. It's a bodily function. But why couldn't she keep it contained to the toilet bowl? Exactly why did she have to display it on the walls and the floor? And exactly how did she get it on the walls and the floor? *Was she dancing?*

So yes, to that lady, Yes, I think you made a mess in the ladies room.

And why do you ladies flush everything down the toilet? Do you flush everything down the toilet at home? Simple rule: toilets that are in restaurants are a lot like toilets at home. We don't have magic "loos" that can act like garbage disposals. If it can't go down the toilet at home, it can't go down the toilet in a restaurant. This is not rocket science.

Another woman came in, used the bathroom, came to make her purchase and we asked her, "How are you?"

"Better now," she replied. "But I just clogged your toilet," she said with a smile.
Oh, goody-goody gum drops!

I like being "outside the box." I like using untraditional signage that doesn't read ladies room or men's room. We have a picture of Wonder Woman on the ladies bathroom door and a picture of Batman on the men's bathroom door. You wouldn't believe how many people need to stop and try to figure out which door they are supposed to use. They stand there and with this puzzled look on their face swaying their head from side to side as if asking themselves which door, this one or that one, this one or that one.

Which picture do you associate more with? Which picture does your body look more like? Do you have breasts like Wonder Woman or do you have a penis like Batman? *This really is a simple thing.*

I made it! Its closing time on Wednesday and we just locked up the restaurant and I'm on my way to the Holistic Studies Institute. (HSI offers holistic studies, reiki, therapeutic touch, and message circles—séances.) I usually take Union Street to Balltown Road then the rest of the way down Central Avenue. Listening to the radio, whenever a happy or message song comes on, I sing my brains out. Thank God nobody is listening to me screaming my lungs out to Natasha Bedingfield's "*Unwritten.*" *There's a sight!*

After some of the days I have I need all the meditation I can get. I release all my negative energy back to the universe. Here, take these thoughts, I don't want them. The trials and tribulations of the day are now out of my hands. So Wednesday nights are my soul cleansing night. I always look forward to being in a room with like-minded people, all wanting the same wisdom.

We start off in quiet time where we sit in silence in the dark and concentrate on our breathing. After that we use pranayamas (a breathing technique) then we repeat our mantra to ourselves and before you know it, we're off in la-la land. It's like a full-mind massage. After our meditation, the instructor leads us in a lecture of the week's topic and we usually have a class participation activity where we learn to develop our intuition and psychic abilities. We learn the difference between psychics and mediums. How learn to see and read people's auras, how to feel spirit energy and how to communicate with loved ones who have crossed over.

That's what brought me there. I would feel this feeling like someone was watching me. Or I had dreams that came true. I would hear a voice in my mind saying to slow down and then a deer would jump out from the side of the road. I know all of these things have happened to everyone. But we all like to pass them off to imagination. It's an easier explanation.

CHAPTER 10

Red Shoes
What's Really Going
Through Their Minds

My buddy Greggie came to me one day and said, "I've been noticing that crazy people wear red shoes."

My first thought was, Red shoes, Um? I thought of Dorothy from *The Wizard of Oz*. She was given red shoes. Fabulous ones, I might add. And the bitch is in "Oz" with flying monkeys, witches and talking trees. Now I ask, does that sound like a normal and well-balanced person to you? I never really noticed red shoes before, but I have to say I do take notice now. Like the movie *The Sixth Sense*, I have a seventh sense. I see crazy people.

Fancy Alice came in and asked, "Can I pay in pennies? I have three dollars in pennies. Pennies, pennies, pennies! My pretty pennies!" *Singing like she was in a Broadway play.* She pulled out her little clear baggie of pennies and held them up for the world to see. Her baby's breath was left for dead, dangling from her disarray hair style. And on her feet were red sandals.

"Well, you better start counting Alice, this could take some time."

We have a customer who believes that he is a nutritionist. Another customer, Jessica, is a little girl—young and trim.

This self-declared nutritionist obviously felt differently. He said to Jessica, "You should eat a sandwich and put on some weight." He took another swig of his beer and felt proud of his rhetorical prognosis. *Thanks for your expert opinion.*

I need to pay more attention to when the moon is full the night before, or if the moon will be full that evening. More often then not, we seem to see an irregular amount of crazed and demented people several times a day and then they disappear for a few weeks and it starts all over again. I've never understood this process. Does it tie in with the government issuing unemployment checks? We do see a lot of "different" people the first of every month. Usually by the 3rd of every month, they've spent their money and are back to pan-handling. The musical instruments come out and they sing and dance for quarters the rest of the month. This is just my observation I'm trying to figure out.

Bacon, bacon, bacon. I love bacon.

Its morning and Stacy went over to a table of two women. This one woman had dark hair, a frizzy-home-dye job with a parted gray line right down the center of her head, blue eye shadow and red lipstick. (I couldn't see her shoe color from where I was in the kitchen.) She ordered her breakfast and said to Stacy, "French toast with two sides of bacon." That wasn't enough. She went on to say, "I can eat a pound of bacon, I just love it," gleaming at Stacy with her wide-open eyes and a full grill of teeth.

Stacy stood there, looking confused, and said, "Did I need to know this?"

Minutes later the woman pushes her purse away from her and into the middle of the walkway. Stacy asked her why. "It was barking at me, so I put it over there."

When Stacy told me this explanation I said to her, "Would she like a bowl of water for her purse?"

Another customer asked if we had "caffeine-filled biscuits" for breakfast. *I'm sure that would get them lining up in the mornings.*

After eating her breakfast, this woman came up to the register and said, "Do I have to pay for another coffee if I want one to go?" *Somebody ate her bowl of stupid this morning.*

A customer came to us one day with a question that really seemed to be nagging at him. He paused for a moment then quietly asked. "If you had to fart, would you tell anyone or would you just fart?" *I know there are people in this world who can help him answer such questions. We're not them.*

A plump woman who came into Ambition using her outside voice proceeded to tell us that she was a purist and didn't like chemicals. She wanted to know if our chai tea was all natural. We let her know that it was. We informed her that it was actually made here in Schenectady by Divini-tea, a local maker and distributor of fine organic teas.

"Great," she yelled, slamming her open palms on the counter with excitement. Then she proceeded to tell us little tidbits of information about herself and her life that we didn't need to know. Would you need to know that she was just released from a psychiatric ward? She told us she was there because she's friends with a fox and several birds that came from outer space visiting her at the bus station. They talk to her and she talks back and nobody believes her. She asks us if we can hear them. *Oh yeah lady, loud and clear! Here's your chai tea, enjoy it, it's on us.*

Finally, she decided to leave the counter for what seemed like an eternity to enter the lounge. As she was walking away, I peered over the bar. Sure enough—red shoes. I thought for sure this woman was going to break out into "*Maniac*," that song from *Flashdance*, spinning herself around and tapping her feet. But please just don't do the dumping of the water bucket part, at least not in the restaurant. Dance all you want outside.

Breakfast that morning was finally over and I was leaving the kitchen with a load of breakfast goods, heading for the walk-in cooler, getting ready to end breakfast and start lunch. My seventh sense went haywire. A man came walking in. I stopped in my tracks and looked at him. Clearly he was a little out of his mind. (Do you know that look? It's something in the eyes that speaks I'm on too many meds or not enough meds. Either way, he did have the "*Eye of The Tiger*.")

He was walking like Mr. Fast Walker, bee-lining for the bathroom. He approached with a mission. I jumped on my game and just stopped with this load of food. *I'm now standing like a quarter-backer ready to take him out.* This man all of a sudden stops and asks, "Excuse me, what day is today?"

I looked to Maria. Maria looked at Jeremy. Jeremy looked to Stacy. We all looked at each other. Stacy took the ball and ran, "It's Monday!"

"Oh, thank you," the man said and left.

Alan, my Sysco food salesman was sitting at high top nearby for that little incident. As he sat there laughing, I too am laughing, so I turned to him and said, "Welcome to my world," while I finished carrying the breakfast food back to the walk-in cooler shaking my head trying to make sense.

Just when we thought we filled our crazy quota for the day, later that afternoon, a young couple came into Ambition and asked, "Do you know of a sandwich shop here on Jay Street?"

Stacy looked at the young woman who was asking the question and, a bit confused, she said, "Yeah, here. We're a sandwich shop. Would you like to see our menu?"

"No, we're going to keep walking around," the young lady said and they left.

About ten minutes later they came back in. They asked us, "Are there any open sandwich shops on Jay Street?"

Stacy looked at her now even more confused then she was ten minutes ago and said again, "Yes, we're open and we're a sandwich shop." Obviously still not believing Stacy, this young couple left again. *Could somebody please carve an "ID" in her forehead for "I'm Dumb."*

A customer said to us, "My coffee is cold."

Quick on her feet and with a comment, Stacy looked to see why it was cold. She replied, "Your coffee is 'white' from all the half and half you used."

"Oh," the customer said. "Well can I dump some out and have more coffee added to warm it up?"

"Only if you don't add anymore half and half," Stacy said.

We get strange people who carry on loud conversations with their friends a lot here. Maria came back into the kitchen one day, laughing and I asked, "What's so funny?"

She said, "There are two ladies in the lounge and one said to the other, 'Oooh, this place is so cute we have to remember and come back.'

"I have no idea how cute it is," replied her friend, "I don't have my glasses on, I can't see." *If only she had her glasses on we might have had a customer for life.*

Phobic people. The world is made up of people with all kinds of phobias.

We have a lady who comes in who has a problem with germs. She'll hand you the money but ask you to put the change on the counter so your hands don't touch hers. (The money has more germs on it than my hands, sweetie.) Then, she'll ask to see your hands to inspect for cuts to make sure she doesn't get any germs that way.

Now her latest tactic is to wear gloves all the time. We asked her, "So where were your gloves last, and are they clean?"

We take it upon ourselves to protect ourselves from her. When we see her come in, we put on gloves too. We ask her to put the money on the counter. And we put her change on the counter so we don't touch her gloves. I think Toby Keith is needed here, *"How Do You Like Me Now!"*

People often give me their opinion on how to operate Ambition. I guess I'm not doing such a good job. Everyone is smarter then I am when it comes to daily operating procedures. Having such a great iconic role model like Madonna, I've heard her accept criticism and roll it off by saying, "Who are you and what are your credentials?"

What gives these people the right to open up their mouth and spew information that they have no formal training of or have been awarded a certificate to prove they're worthy of an opinion.

Friday, June 8th, 2:36 p.m., the phone rang, and I picked it up. "Ambition, Marc speaking," is how I usually answer the phone. I like to know with whom I'm speaking with so I give my name hoping to get a name back. That didn't happen. A woman said she'd like to make a complaint. Oh boy, I think. What happened now?

"Whenever my friend and I come there, our bread is never grilled. The menu says grilled, but it's not. It's just dry toast. That's not grilled."

"We don't use butter when grilling our sandwiches. This makes them less greasy," hoping to win her over, but I didn't.

"Well, then, it's not grilled. You should grill your sandwiches if your menu says grilled."

"So your sandwich today wasn't grilled?" I asked her.

"I'm not talking about today. I'm talking about every time we come in, the bread isn't grilled," she answered.

"When *was* the last time you were here?"

"A month ago, she answered."

This was one of those moments when I needed to take a deep breath because I was starting to get agitated. I was thinking of what type of person would call a restaurant *a month later* to complain because the sandwiches aren't grilled with butter. Meanwhile as she blathered on, it hit me. I heard her speech and it slowed down then she slurred, repeated herself, and then slurred again. All of a sudden, fireworks went off in my mind and I realized... *this lady is drunk.*

Cancer the Crab, Snap! "So you were here a month ago and decided to call and complain, today?" I asked. My inner Mister Facetious stepped forward and now took over the conversation. I said to her, "Well, if you want to go the fat route, we can butter and grill your sandwiches for you the next time you come in. Just tell us to do so. But you'll need to tell us because we don't butter the bread."

"Well then, if you don't use butter, it's still not grilled," she said.

I'm done! My last nerve was just used, and I'm now going for the jugular. "Ma'am," I said, "I think you've had too much to drink today!"

Silence.

"Fuck you! Fuck you! Fuck you! If you don't listen to me, your business will fail, and I hope your year will be terrible," she said.

"That's not gonna happen. I'm protected in positive white light," I said to her.

"Fuck you, fuck you," she said.

"Well, you can say that, but my positive white light, you can't destroy," I said. Then I hear, CLICK!

The phone rang again in less than two minutes, and a bit shaken I grabbed it again and answered, "Ambition, Marc speaking."

Oh, that lovely voice came over the receiver again, the one I now know so well, and said, "Your business is in trouble because of this, and you'll have a terrible year. I mean it," she said.

Now I knew whom I was dealing with, and I'm actually starting to get amused by this conversation. "No, I won't. I'm protected by positive white light, and you can't harm me," I said.

"Fuck you, fuck you," she said, CLICK!

Four minutes later after the second phone call, now at 2:54 p.m. the phone rang again. This time Maria, who didn't believe the conversation I just had with little Miss Wine-O, answered the phone. "Ambition, Maria speaking."

This woman now proceeded to tell Maria how our sandwiches aren't grilled, stating her professional matter of fact, "You'll lose customers if you don't start grilling the sandwiches."

Maria responded, "Well, there are a lot of people who like what we do here and how we grill our sandwiches. You're the first person to complain about our method of grilled sandwiches and I know—I've worked here for many years."

"I want you to tell your boss he needs to listen to me and grill the sandwiches and that's all I'll say," she said. But wait, she had more to say. "By the way, tell your boss that the food is over priced and you're understaffed. I hope he listens to me." Again click. *Who knows, maybe she finished the bottle and went for more?*

So now this brings me to, why do I get all the "fuck you's?"

The phone rang and I answered, "Ambition, Marc speaking." CLICK! Okay, wrong number, I thought, and went back to doing what I was doing. Forty-five seconds later the phone rang again, "Ambition, Marc speaking." Again, CLICK! Now, I was pissed. You've just hung up in my ear twice, and you've interrupted me now, twice. You're stupid. So I dial *69. I retrieved the last number, which just called fifty-seven seconds ago and I dialed.

Well, surprise, the caller was no longer home, only a minute and twenty seconds later. So I waited for the answering machine to pick up. And it did. On came this little girl's voice being prompted by her mother *(whisper)* leave a message and we'll call you back, so the little girl's voice repeats, leave a message and we'll call you back. Beeeepp!

So I did. I said, "My name is Marc. I own Ambition and you've just called my restaurant twice. Both times you hung up in my ear. I would appreciate it if, in the future, you said, oh, I'm sorry, I dialed the wrong number, instead of just hanging up in my ear." I ended it with, "thank you, have a great day."

Well, four minutes later, the phone rang. Surprise, guess who it is? Yes, she's home again and it's Miss Congeniality. She than asked if I was the person who just left a message on her answering machine.

I said, "Yes."

She then goes on to tell me the reason she hung up both times was that her daughter was playing with the phone and disconnected the line, twice.

So I asked her, "Is there something you'd like to ask me now that you have me?"

"Well, not now, I'll never call your business again."

"Oh, okay, thank you," I said.

She went on to say that I should pay more attention to running my business instead of calling people back and lecturing them about proper phone etiquette.

"Thank you for that advice."

At this point she was pissed that I kept thanking her, so she dug a little more and said, "I would think that if you ran a successful restaurant you wouldn't have time to call people back and harass them but your business mustn't be that good if you have all that free time."

I said, "We do very well here, thank you."

She said, "No, thank you!"

I followed with, "Thank you!"

Then came the, "fuck you, fuck you!" CLICK! *I think somebody needs a bar of Ivory soap in their mouth.*

We had a bachelor party in the restaurant after hours and the guests brought in a stripper. Okay. Whatever. The stripper got butt naked in the lounge. She took the men's ties, danced and wiggled, did what a stripper does with men's ties, if you're with me, (if not, she uses them *like* dental floss, only in another area.) The party ended and all the men left happy, I'm very sure of this.

The next day, who showed up? None other than our Little Miss Stripper. She politely asked, because I believe there's no other way to go about it, if we had found her panties. They were missing, and she was wondering where they were. If we were to find them (she gave me her number) she wanted us to call her. *Sweetie, I'm sure after that little dental floss trick, those panties are long gone with one of the boys!*

It has come to my attention that crazy people who don't wear red shoes sit in our booth #1. It's right there at the door. They usually sit in it when the restaurant is completely empty. They sit facing the door with their backs toward us. I don't understand this little ritual of how all these people learned this procedure, but it happens quite often, at least enough times to make this part of the chapter. Why do they do this? It can't be comfortable to be so far from everything else and with your back toward the world. Wouldn't you want to know if the server sees you? If you don't face us, how do you know we saw you? So then these people start turning around looking at us as if to say, here I am. Do you see me? Just move closer in the restaurant to a more central location and enjoy your visit.

We all fall in love with a new partner at one time or another. Starting a new romance, what a wonderful feeling it is. But being in love should be left at home. I would never go into a restaurant, sit in the lounge and suck face with my new lover while the waitress is trying to take my order. *Is this a bad time? Should I come back? Can I bring you a cigarette when you're done?* Where's the sense of decorum in these people? Do they think we want to see them sucking face? Keep it at home or get a motel room. Maybe I should put "brothel" on the web site. *The building once was. Like attracts like.*

Phantom of the Opera was in town for a three-week run at Proctor's, and we had a cast party for the crew. These parties are always fun because the casts get wild. They drink, sing and dance. The music is loud, the energy levels are high and everyone is bumping and grinding with everyone. Then we have some guests like the two boys who disappeared into the men's bathroom for twenty minutes. One could only wonder what went on in there. *Oh, Bula, you're still working your magical touch.*

Touchy subject, the human body, but when a man is happy something happens to…a…uh…a *certain* part of the body. Am I clear enough with this one? So when this happens in a restaurant, you'd think the man would stay seated until his… happiness is over. Oh, but not here in Schenectady. Just parade your *happiness* throughout the place. This man fell asleep in the lounge. He woke up and took a walk through the restaurant with his Uncle Jimmy. He was long and narrow and so is our restaurant. He had quite the cat walk from the lounge to the door. Reminds me of Cole Porter's song, "*Love For Sale.*"

Now, if your Uncle Jimmy visited you, would you stand up from one table and go over to another and proceed to talk, (hello, hi there, salute, raise the flagpole) to a family of four, two of whom are small children? Welcome to Schenectady. Maria and I were mortified that day. *Few things shock me anymore but this was one of them.*

A woman came in and stole the adult section of a weekly free paper, stating, "The pictures and articles are against God." She thought that particular section was disgusting and no one needed to see that. Thank you for deciding for us all and taking it upon yourself to protect us from damnation. So my wait staff cornered her and made her return the papers and leave. We haven't seen her lately. *Maybe she's at church repenting.*

Baby Jane came in one day for a sandwich. She usually wears pink shoes (pink is a shade of red), sky blue pants, a yellow shirt, a peach scarf around her neck, and some sort of beach hat. If she isn't wearing a beach hat, her red hair is usually teased to maximum obstruct ability. A tornado couldn't move her hair. Her makeup is in the style of Betty Davis in *Whatever Happened to Baby Jane?* She has full painted red lips, circles of blush on her cheeks, blue eye shadow and lots of eyeliner. *Maybelline must love her.*

She sat down and Jeremy took her order. Her option was the build your own sandwich. She wanted multi grain bread, roast beef, provolone and all the toppings. All the toppings consist of lettuce, tomatoes, black olives, jalapenos, red onions, sprouts, carrots, green peppers, roast red peppers and cucumbers. Baby Jane started eating her sandwich and called Jeremy over. He approached and asked, "How is everything?"

She said, with great big eyes and gleaming teeth, nodding, "Great, but I didn't get sprouts!" She kept on smiling and nodding.

Jeremy then asked, "Would you like to have sprouts put on your sandwich?"

"No," she said, taking a breath and still smiling. "I just wanted you to know." She nodded affirmatively. *What is it with Jeremy's customers and sprouts?*

A woman came in one Wednesday afternoon, and Jeremy was behind the bar. Now this was when Jeremy had just started, and he wasn't yet up to speed with the menu, with the drinks, *or the crazies*, so I stepped out of the kitchen and greeted her. I told her the specials of the day and she told me she wanted a nutty Irishman. (This is an espresso beverage we offer with Irish cream, hazelnut syrup and a shot of Bushmills in it.) Jeremy made the drink, and the lady started drinking it. She was still reading the menu, so Jeremy said, "Have you made any decisions yet?" Now, mind you, Jeremy, is a charmer, *yeah, he flirts*, and his overall philosophy is whatever makes you happy, as he throws his shoulders up and raises his hands and arms in a "whatever" motion.

So this woman asked, "Is the soup vegetarian?" The soup was split pea that day.

Jeremy said, "Yes."

Then she said she's a vegetarian, and she's looking at all of our options. Jeremy started mentioning our green street, the black bean burger, the build your own sandwich option, and she interrupted him and said, "I need another minute."

About ten minutes later her face was still in the menu. I looked at Jeremy and said, "What's she doing, it's a menu not a novel!" Five more minutes went by, and she finally decided she didn't want anything to eat. She paid for her drink and walked back to the lounge.

Now my *freak alert* was beeping. I told the wait staff to watch her. So she proceeded to the lounge and opened a door to the liquor room. That door should have been locked, but no normal person ever opened it before. She looked in and closed the door. Then she opened the door to our walk-in cooler, put her face in the cooler, probably felt the cold air, and closed the door.

I stopped her and asked, "What are you doing?"

She looked at me and said, "It doesn't say *Do Not Enter*, and so I wanted to peek inside."

My Cancer the Crab stepped forward and said, "The men's room doesn't say *Do Not Enter*, but that doesn't mean you open it and look in!"

"Oh, I'm sorry. I'll go now," she said.

Yeah, that would be a good idea.

Metroplex bought parking lots from the city and since 2005 it has been charging for parking. Paid parking had never has been implemented in Schenectady before. It caused a big stir in the city with its residents, visitors and employees of small businesses like Ambition. The *Times Union*, a local newspaper, wrote an article on paid parking and took pictures using two of my employees—one being Stacy—for their thoughts on this parking issue. Stacy, as I've described her, is a pretty woman, high cheek bones and, to boot, big boobs. *Hurray, I can hear some of you men yelling… and ladies too!*

After the article ran, about a week later Stacy received a letter from the Schenectady County Jail. Quizzically, Stacy looked at the letter, thinking, who's sending me a letter from the county jail? It was from an inmate who was going to be released from jail in a year or so. He saw Stacy's picture in the newspaper and took it upon himself to profess his innocence of his crime. Writing that he would soon be released, he suggested maybe the two of them could start a relationship so he would have a place to live when he's released. He signed the letter, "Shine on, Tommy!" What a fine catch I'm sure Tommy is. Stacy would be a fool not to accept his proposal. I'm sure many women would jump at an opportunity like this. *Was this already an episode on Jerry Springer? "This man wrote me from jail and now we're married."*

A woman came in dressed all in white lace: lace stocking, lace dress, lace gloves and a white hat to top off her ensemble. We, of course, saw her and thought, *what the hell?* She's as crazy as the day is long.

She sat at the bar and shook salt and pepper into her hand and ate it. She repeated this about three times. Opened sugar packets and ate the sugar. Now I guess she was thirsty because she walked over to the Coke cooler and bought a ginger ale. She sipped it and started pouring it on the counter, laughing and so proud of what she was doing. We jumped into panic mode, cleaned up the mess and started thinking, what is she going to do next? Oh why did we think of that question? Because here it came…

Now she was hungry so she walked over to the *gelato* case and asked to try a sample of every single flavor, one by one. "Can I try the vanilla," giggle, giggle. Then of course the sound effects come, "Mmmmm, Ooohhh, Yeah, that's good! Can I try the raspberry?" Again, the sounds effects, and then on to all 10 other flavors. *This is fun to do and is a great waste of time especially when the restaurant is busy. Super, lady. I really have time for this right now.*

She finally found a flavor she wanted. *The vanilla, her first sample choice…why me?* She took two small spoonfuls with the little plastic spoon that's served with *gelato* and then started pouring her ginger ale over the *gelato.* "I'm making an ice cream soda," she said, as the ginger ale was flowing over the rim of the *gelato* cup and onto the counter. Her eyes all aglow. Her face beaming with excitement. Finishing, she starts clapping at her performance. *One would think she was front row at a Madonna concert.*

As I usually do, I ruined her concert. I'm such a fuddy-duddy; never want to have any fun. I always have to follow the rules. I said to her, "First of all, you need a glass to do that so it doesn't go all over the counter." She laughed with this cackle-like laugh, and then I said, "Miss, we're going to have to ask you to leave."

The look of disappointment in her eyes was horrible. "You, you…you want me to leave?" Her bottom lip started to tremble like she was about to cry, looking all sad like she was just any other typical guest out having lunch with a good friend. "What did I do wrong, why me, what did I say?"

"You said enough, you did enough, thank you for coming in."

Jen, a long time customer, came in one day with her sister. We all acknowledged Jen as being a regular. "Hello Jen." She said hello back to us. But Jen's sister seemed particularly unhappy all of the sudden.

She turned to "Jen" and said, "Joyce! I'm Jen! Stop using my name! Your name is Joyce! I'm going to tell your counselor you're using my name again. Let's see how he likes that! We've been through this before, remember all the credit card bills you ran up in my name, remember that phone bill! You have got to stop this!" The real Jen took Joyce by the arm and whirled her out of the restaurant about as fast as they came in. *Just when you thought you knew someone. For the record, we still call her Jen.*

Think Julia Roberts from the movie, *Pretty Woman*. Do you have the vision? Okay, here we go... *a not-so-pretty-woman* came in and wanted to use the bathroom. We told her it was for customers only, and she needed to buy something. "I will," she said and walked to the bathroom. *Well she strutted to the bathroom for better terms.* Black knee high, spiked boots. Fish net stockings with a rather large hole in the back of the stocking just below her red mini skirt. A white t-shirt ripped from the neckline to her cleavage with a neon pink cheetah bra underneath, carrying her over-sized zebra shoulder bag. *God only knows what toys she had in her bag?* And unfortunately for her, she's not as attractive as Julia Roberts. *Not even close.*

She entered the bathroom and was gone for fifteen minutes.

Other customers now wanted to use the bathroom, but it was "occupied." Her pimp/boyfriend, whoever he was, came in, looked for her and asked, "Where she at?"

I was a little surprised that Mr. Bling, who was now standing in front of me with his gold tooth, red suede gym suit and black sneakers would just assume I would know who he was speaking of in a packed restaurant. Somehow, I did. Needless to say, they somehow both managed to stand out quite boldly in Ambition.

"In the bathroom," I told him.

"She bin gone fifteen minute now," he said.

"We all know," I said.

Our happy hooker finally came out all showered, changed *(but still in her boots)* and perfumed, ready for her next day of work. I can say "perfumed" because nothing fills the air of a restaurant quite like cheap perfume. She bought her coffee and they both left. *I never knew we were the YMCA or the YWCA, for that matter. I'll be sure to put that on our website, too.*

An older couple came in for breakfast Wednesday morning and Stacy is their waitress. Stacy chit-chats with them a little and the man went outside to smoke a cigarette. The woman proceeded to tell Stacy that they both live at the "Y." She said, "I live at the woman's Y and he lives at the men's Y. They have a delicious breakfast for $4.95 at the men's Y. That's where we met." This woman went on to say, "You know I used to wash dishes at Woolworth's—in the basement—making tips, but I needed to share my tips with the other dishwashers so I quit. Do you need help here?" She started to laugh, "I'm only joking darling, I don't want a job, Social Security pays me just fine."

She finished her food and cleared the table of its dishes and said, "Now where's your garbage darling and dish cart? See, I can wait tables too!" She laughed and was very proud of her abilities. She sat back down and her boyfriend was still outside smoking so she called Stacy over with a curl of her finger, "Pssst, come here honey, I've got something to tell you. That man out there, mmm…the things he does to me, mmm! I can't wait for tonight! He's equipped!" She puts her hands on her breasts, gives them a good squeeze and lets out another sigh, aaaahhhh! She reaches for her purse and she pulls out a picture of "how equipped" he is.

Stacy came directly to the kitchen, embarrassed and shocked but acknowledged that she looked because she said; "I didn't believe she would actually show me a picture of his dick."

Fortunately for Stacy, and saved by the bells on the door, the man came back in and she was spared from any more juicy details. *I asked Stacy if she was going to subscribe to the new magazine, Dirty, Homeless and hung.*

It was 9:30 a.m. on a Tuesday and an older woman came in with a strong accent asking for a glass of chardonnay. She was dressed nicely, short dark hair, make up, purse and cane in hand. Maria brought her a wine glass and took her breakfast order. *Yes, you're reading this correctly: breakfast order.*

Maria brought the order to the kitchen, which is fifteen steps from the bar. Then we heard the sound of a glass hitting the bar. We looked at her, and her now empty wine glass. I looked at Maria and she at me. Both of us rolled our eyes.

Nothing else needed to be said. The woman asked for another glass of chardonnay. Maria filled another glass and brought it to her while whispering a few Spanish words of repent for the woman. Chugging it the same way, the woman slapped her empty glass down on the bar. *Maybe offering a straw may have slowed her down.*

Now that she was properly self-medicated, she ordered a "little Italy" which is espresso with a shot of Sambuca. She received her caffeine-filled xanax along with a breakfast sandwich, which she began to eat. While she was enjoying her sandwich and odd breakfast beverage, her therapist walked in and saw her.

"Oh, good morning!" the therapist said to her. "Enjoying your breakfast and coffee?" I know this is her therapist because I know what this man does for a living. I know that when he announces his presence to a guest that he knows them well. *And because I'm so smart, I can put two and two together and get four. Guilty by association.* This woman responded, "Everything is just delicious" and belched. As she belched, a piece of her egg sandwich fell out of her mouth and on to the counter. *In Japan, that's a compliment.*

One day an old drunk came in and asked if we sell beer by the gallon. *Thirsty little fella, aren't you?*

It's July, and one of our usual customers came in. He looked at the specials board, read the soup, which was watermelon gazpacho and the list of ingredients. Its base is watermelon but we also add mangoes, grapes, strawberries, limes and apples. Then he turned to me and asked, "Can you take the watermelon out of the watermelon gazpacho?"

I closed my eyes, bowed my head, and put my palm on my forehead and started to rub it like a headache was coming on, and mumbled "why me?" I opened my eyes again and I couldn't do or say anything else besides laugh.

He saw my look and he started to laugh also. Then he said, "My head just exploded! I should just go outside and come back in, and start all over again, shouldn't I."

An otherwise normal looking woman came in and asked, "What do you have that's hot to drink?" Stacy, taken off guard, started listing all the coffees, then teas, then stopped... and realized how stupid of a question it was.

Stacy came in the kitchen and said, "Just give me a wall to beat my head against."

Stacy greeted a man at the bar and he ordered a coffee. Then he yelled, "With cream!"

A little shocked by the sudden outburst, I said to Stacy, "Did you hear he wants cream with his coffee?" I was joking, of course. They probably heard him in Mexico.

Coolly, Stacy just smiled at the man after his comment, her big mistake.

So the man yelled again, "With cream!"

Stacy whipped around at him and said this time, "Yes, I heard you the first time, you want cream!" *Yell again, and you'll be wearing the cream!*

Ambition is gay-owned, so, of course we're gay friendly. For anyone not familiar with this term, it means gay people can come in and feel comfortable in the ambiance of Ambition. Two men, two ladies, what have you. We advertise in gay publications in the Tri-city region, of Albany, Schenectady and Troy.

Two men walked in one Saturday and looked oddly at the place. They walked through the restaurant and into the lounge. As they were coming back through, I stopped them and said, "Hello men, how can we help you?" Gay people recognize other gay people by means of gaydar. (Gaydar is an internal homing beacon that signals the presence of gayness.) And most of us have seen *Will & Grace*.

So they said to me, "We saw your ad for Ambition in *Q-magazine* (a gay publication) and it sounded like a sex shop to us. We were wondering if you had a dungeon." He was still smiling. (If you're not aware, a private sex room in a basement of a building is called a dungeon.

I explained we do serve adult beverages and we don't have a children menu but to infer from that, that we are an adult store...

"Oh, okay," they said and left.

If only we offered a dungeon, we would have what all men what most, sex and food.

Above the kitchen's entrance is a "men's room" sign. There's also a sign that says *Danger Men Cooking*. There's a picture of Lynda Carter as *Wonder Woman*. The whole joke here is when we started the restaurant, only men were working in the kitchen. For no reason at all it just worked out that way. So I played off of that with the signs. I could tell you that if it happened once, it happened a hundred times. Men would just walk into the kitchen and look for the bathroom. They see me standing there and ask, "Where is it?"

I used to respond, "Where's what?" but figured I could accept a small dose of my own medicine. If you're going to hang a "men's room" sign above the doorway to the kitchen I guess I should expect men to come in and look for the bathroom.

Two women came in one afternoon and the one looked at the other: "Men's room," she said pointing, "They go to the bathroom in the kitchen. That's nasty!"

"No, only a dumb ass like *you* would think that!" her friend casually responded.

Coupons. We all use them. But there are *rules* for using coupons. So why is it that when a customer comes in with a coupon for "up to five dollars off," they expect change for anything less then five dollars?

One customer just didn't get why she wasn't getting any money back after buying a coffee because her coupon read $5.00 off. Would someone please explain this one to her? It's a coupon, not a gift certificate. The coupon read 50% off up to $5.00 on any item. Can it read any clearer?

What about the six people who come in with three coupons and ask for separate checks. If you're that short on cash, why are you eating out?

Then there are the customers who bring in three different coupons and expect to use them all at once. "Buy one drink, get one free," and "enjoy a free coffee on us," and our ever popular

"$5.00 off" coupon. Why do these people expect to come into the restaurant and get one drink for free, then get $5.00 off their meal, and finish with a free coffee? The coupons read, "Only one coupon per table, and not to be used with any other offer. What's going through these people's minds? Coupons are a slow descent into madness. *I don't think I could ever work the early bird specials in Florida. How do they do it?*

One morning a man walked into the restaurant. The lights were off. The sign on the front door read, "Closed." He walked in and said, "The sign on the front door reads closed, the lights are off but you're in here... I was wondering if you're really actually closed?"

"Yes," I replied, "we're really actually closed."

"Would you like me to leave?" he asked.

I looked at his shoes...red. "Yes," I answered.

I guess I should nail boards over the front door until we open. Would that make things easier?

You'd be surprised how often the older red shoed men ask Stacy and Maria their old-timely question, "Is your boyfriend disposable?" *Why is it that men think it's acceptable to do this? Do they really think it's gonna work?*

I've never once heard either of them reply in the affirmative. Yes, I'm a pretty twenty-year-old. You're a drunken, perverted, sixty-year-old grumpier old man. Match made in heaven. *Hang on a sec; let me drop my boyfriend in the dumpster out back so we can get friendly.*"

A woman entered Ambition right at noon on a Sunday. We're normally closed, but *Mamma Mia* was in town so we opened to cater to the theater crowd. This woman was on the chunky side. She was of Hispanic descent with olive skin. Wearing a pullover sweatshirt, jeans and baseball cap.

She asked Jeremy if he spoke Spanish. He doesn't—Maria was off that day. Then she asked if he spoke French. He doesn't. Then she asked Jeremy, if he would be her friend.

Jeremy now knows he's going to have his hands full with her, so he came into the kitchen and told me what was going on.

Making sure not to send the wrong message, I thought the most delicate way to handle the situation was to say that "We're only here to offer you coffee and food. How about a cup of coffee?"

"Sure."

It worked!

He poured the cup of coffee, placed it on the counter in front of her and said, "$1.85, please."

"I'm not sure I want the coffee now. Can I just sit here?"

Understand that I dislike working Sundays. To start the day off like this put me in a foul mood. So I walked out of the kitchen being very much me, and I was quick to the point. "Either you buy the coffee and sit in the lounge or you leave. Which one will it be?" *Cancer the Crab, Snap!*

She then asked me, "Do you speak Spanish?"

(Being in Schenectady for many years I've learned to deal with these insane people. Don't have conversations with them. Give them yes or no questions and that's it. Don't give them the room to ask questions). I said, "That's not the question. Buy the coffee or leave! What will it be?"

She then asked, "Will you be my friend?"

"Nope, sorry. Buy the coffee or leave."

"So, if I buy the coffee can I stay?"

"Yes".

"But I don't want the coffee."

I let my guard down and started a conversation with her. "I'll count to ten in Spanish and you'll be out of here or I'm going to have to call the police. "*Uno, dos, tres,*" I said. I got to *diez* and she lit up like a Christmas tree. A great wide smile, those theatrical shining eyes... I thought she was going to break out into, "*I'm So Pretty,*" from *West Side Story*.

"Do you speak French?" she asked excitely.

"Ok. I have to call the police." I called and she just sat there staring at me.

A woman answered, "Hello, Schenectady police."

"Yes, my name is Marc from Ambition on Jay Street. I have a woman here who is refusing to leave and we think she might be some trouble." That's when Miss Do You Speak Spanish got up and walked toward the door. I said to the woman on the line, "Oh, she's leaving now. But would you please wait on the line until she's out of the building?" The dispatcher started laughing; I started laughing. "It's going to be one of those days."

Miss Do You Speak Spanish walked out the door and was gone. I said, "thank you" to the dispatcher and hung up.

Three days later, Miss Do You Speak Spanish was standing at the front door, waving from the outside at us with a big smile on her face. She flapped her hands around and walked away. That was hopefully the last we will ever see of her again.

I feel compelled to add that when I first heard this verbal observation of red shoes and what red shoes indicated about the people wearing them, I went home and, to my surprise (but probably not yours,) I have three pairs of red shoes, *uh-ohh*.

CHAPTER 11

Nail It, Glue It or Screw It

Growing up and working at my parents many businesses, I've heard my father say, "Nail it, glue it or screw it!" a million times. The quote never made too much sense to my twelve-year old mind. Now that I own a business of my own, I understand the relevance of this statement.

We have a *Wonder Woman* figurine (I love her) from a garage sale, which probably cost me a dollar. One day, a lady and her friend came in to buy some coffee. They saw *Wonder Woman* on the coffee counter where she was placed and preceded to take it off the counter and put it on their table. *The gauntlet has been thrown down.* "You like *Wonder Woman?*" I asked.

"Yeah," she laughed.

I didn't understand at the moment why she laughed, but I went with it, and thought maybe she was just a little embarrassed for liking *Wonder Woman*.

I walked away but told my employees... watch her. After she and her friend finished their coffee, they got up to leave. But when I looked quickly at her table, then at the coffee counter, not a single, satin tights, nor those stars and stripes could be found. I reached for my golden lasso.

"Um, excuse me. That, uh, *Wonder Woman* figurine is ours," I said.

The one girl seemed quite a bit uncomfortable. After some hesitating, she opened her purse and revealed *Wonder Woman* stuck inside. "I... thought they were for sale?"

"Well, then, shouldn't you have you paid for it?" *One stupid response deflected with my bracelets.*

"Oh, I guess I forgot too," she said.

So, now *Wonder Woman* is still in the building but she's firmly affixed to the coffee station with glue.

I doubt that even *The Bionic Woman* would be able to get away with her now. They'll have to drag the Hoosier cabinet out with them and I don't think I'll miss that being dragged out the front door.

Madonna, my other superhero. There are many Madonna pictures throughout the restaurant. Yes, even in the men's room. I thought the patrons would enjoy it while "standing" taking care of business. It's a picture of the Material Girl taken by Herb Ritts for Andy Warhol's magazine *Interview* from June 1990. She's bending forward, holding her breasts, wearing fish net stockings, panties and a great pair of stilettos. No nudity, just imagination.

One day someone took the picture right out of the frame.

Four shady looking men were sitting at table #9. I say shady here because you can tell the difference between someone who wants help for an addiction and someone who wants to avoid going to jail. So these people are enlisted usually in court appointed rehab, *it's certainly not voluntary*, they do their appointed time, then they're free to go back out into society and this entitles them permission to do it all over again, *on tax payers money.*

So I know my customers, and I knew exactly which table it was that did it.

About a week later, a couple of the same people came in again. So, little 5' 8" gay me, goes up to the table and said to them, "Tell your friend who stole the Madonna picture out of the bathroom to come back in here so I can kick his ass."

Well, that didn't go over to well. One replied, "You don't know who you're talking to. You don't know what I can do and what connections I have. You should shut your mouth."

I was scared, but didn't show it. (Well, a little more than scared, to be honest. But I wasn't going to let this crack head steal out of my restaurant.) And I also wanted it to be known, I didn't want them in the restaurant. So I stood there and repeated myself, "You just go tell your friend that I know." I had a sick feeling that a brick would go through my window. You know how resourceful these kinds of people can be. So far, nothing else happened, and that particular picture remained missing until I came across another copy of *Interview* magazine about three years. So, Madonna, once again, is in the men's bathroom in all her glory. But this time it's a copy of the picture and not the original. *"You Learn"* Thanks, Alanis! I need to add that this Madonna picture has now been stolen out of the frame from the men's bathroom, *twice. Xerox is my new best friend.* So now what I've done is screwed the picture to the wall. *I haven't replaced it since.*

People love to drink martinis. On top of being tasty, they look fetchingly fun in that glass. We had images of Marilyn Monroe by Andy Warhol on martini glasses. Hence the past tense here, *we had*. Apparently some customers who ordered martinis liked the glasses as much as we did. Or maybe they thought the glasses were included with the purchase. We still have tasty martinis but the funky glasses are long gone.

A woman came in and bought a cup of coffee. She put her money down on the same cabinet that the wait staff uses to write orders, pick up food and count their tips. There was a dollar bill folded up on that counter sitting there. She got her coffee, collected her change, *and* snatched the extra buck. As you probably know, I'm not too shy of a guy so I said to the woman, "You just took that dollar."

Stuttering, "No, no, I uh, I didn't," she responded.

I said, "Open your wallet and there will be a dollar bill in there folded up."

She opened her wallet. There it was.

"I, um, I thought it was my change."

"I thought you said that you didn't take it? Then you said, I thought it was part of my change. Ah, I see an easy mistake." *As my Grandmother Renson would have said, "Clear as mud."*

We have a tambourine, a maraca, and an accordion right next to the register. These instruments are there for the sole purpose of putting a smile on a person's face. I call it "Instant Smile." Someone shakes it, they smile; it's that simple. Besides being right under our noses, these three instruments are tied to the register with plastic straps. Somebody stole the accordion. First of all, how did they do it right under our noses? And second, why would someone steal a $12 plastic accordion? It's not a particularly glamorous musical instrument... or is it?

A woman came in and made change out of the "tips" bowl at the register. Who does this? Who has enough nerve to go to a "tips bowl" and make change without asking? Another problem was that she didn't put as much money in as she took out. She got caught. I like to think of myself as the all seeing, all knowing watcher of the shop so, of course, I watched her like a hawk. Not only did she not make change, she helped herself to an extra five dollar bill.

"I saw you take the five dollars."

"No, I, I didn't." She started panicking. She was looking at who was around her, and you could see her mind working as she was trying to think of a way out of this situation.

"Miss," I sighed, "we really don't want you as a customer here anymore. Please don't come back."

She did leave but instead of staying out of my hair she told her parents the whole story, except the truth about her taking the five dollar bill. So her parents came in and asked me what happened and I explained it to them.

"Well," they said, "our daughter is mildly retarded but we don't think she would do something like that."

"I'm sure she wouldn't in your presence. But I know what I saw. Your daughter took that money."

"Can you forgive her?" they pleaded. "This is her favorite place."

"The only way I would forgive her is if she comes in with supervision," I said.

Although we never saw her in again, I still see her on the streets, still unsupervised. You go girl!

I bought an antique, red-glass, Italian-made ashtray for the outside of the restaurant. New York State is smoke-free almost everywhere so smoking is not allowed in restaurants or in any public spaces for that matter. I brought the ashtray knowing for certain that it would be stolen. After all, it was far too cute for us to hold on to for long. I'm sure someone else would want to take it home.

A person came in one day with a bit of a hang-over. He was carrying quite a load: drums, a guitar and other bags. When he left, he hit the ashtray and knocked it over. The glass smashed to bits and he was gone. Pouring salt onto the wound, he didn't bother to pick it up or even tell us about it. I noticed it smashed on the ground about five minutes after, knowing damn well Mr. Hangover and his load of crap knocked it over.

Ten minutes later, Mr. Hangover is back again for a cup of coffee.

"You came in here earlier with your stuff and…"

"Yeah," he interrupted. "I know, I hit your ashtray, and I broke it. I'm really sorry." He was wiping his face and rubbing his blood-shot eyes because he was so hung-over he could barely keep his eyes open.

"There's not a lot of extra space in here and I don't want you bringing your things in." I wasn't that upset about the ashtray because I thought it was going to be stolen anyways. "But why didn't you tell us you broke it?"

"Yeah, I know," he said. "That was stupid but next door at the church, I play in the band. I need all these instruments. If I can't bring them in anymore, I won't be in anymore either."

Going to church hung-over? My father used this quote on one of his customers at the beauty shop they owned, *"Don't let the door hit you in the ass."*

You can buy mirrors just about anywhere. Why do people steal them out of our bathrooms? What is it about our mirrors that compel people to steal them? Were they magic and I didn't know it? *Is there a genie inside looking out?* We *had* a sun-shaped mirror in the ladies room and a moon-shaped mirror in the men's room—both lifted.

I've found a great sign for the bathrooms. It reads, "We aim to keep our bathrooms clean. Gentlemen, your aim would help here, stand closer, it's not as long as you think and ladies, please remain seated throughout the entire performance!"
I bought two of these signs and in two days one was lifted. So, I photocopied the original one and replaced the stolen sign. In one week's time the sign was stolen again. Third photocopy... gone in sixty seconds. I feel like I'm living with children. *Can't we have anything nice?*

A Barrel of Monkeys. We have a barrel in the lounge. Guests like to hook each monkey's arm into another, pulling the monkeys out of the barrel all connected in a line. I believe twenty monkeys came in the barrel. The monkeys have slowly gone missing. We now have a barrel with two monkeys in it. Wow, lots of fun. *Could we have our monkeys back, please?*

We added another table to the lounge in 2001 and decided to paint a checkerboard on it. We bought checkers and had happy guests playing checkers, until the day one of our fine upstanding fellow citizens stole the box of checkers. Now the happy guests use sugar packets. You can't keep us down.

Menus. Why do people steal menus? Why not just ask for a paper take-out menu? Better yet, if you feel the need to take a menu, here's an idea, buy one from the restaurant. Guess what, they're expensive to make. And we probably need them more than you.

Salt and pepper shakers. Need I say more? If you noticed on your table that either one was missing, you'll know why.

Silverware. (Especially knives.) I know they get thrown in the garbage by the wait staff when they're in a hurry but when the wait staff clears your table and the silverware is already gone, *better get Sherlock Holmes in on this one.*

Sugar packets. *These are for checkers!* Why do people feel that because they bought a cup of coffee that they're entitled to just shove packets of sugar in their pockets? What is it about sugar packets that people like so much? I should just ask the little old ladies who grab the packets and put them in their purses. Or I could ask the college students. Or should I ask the people who come in and just downright steal the packets without being a customer. *I have a five pound bag of sugar in the kitchen would you like that too?*

Saltines. Does one person really need twenty crackers in a cup of soup? *Would you like a glass of water to wash it all down?*

I like the people who come in and take napkins, plastic forks and spoons. Then they say, "I left mine at home." How about asking if it's okay to take, or better yet, ask to buy them because you forgot yours at home.

Sure, take as many as you want, girl, I got them for free this week! I just clicked on free@ambition and loaded up.

Toilet paper. You didn't! People steal the extra rolls of toilet paper we leave in the bathrooms. *Believe it like the Bible.*

There are those days when I look around the restaurant at all the things that I've had to secure to the walls, cabinets, and doors. I smile and chuckle to myself, pleased with my efforts. (*"Nail it, glue it, or screw it." Thanks mom and dad.*) Then my mind wanders off to the day when Ambition will retire and the happy new owners come in…with a jack hammer to get all this stuff off. (Good luck with our sparkly archway glued with thousands of bottle caps.)

CHAPTER 12

Buckets of Money

Lots of things can go wrong in a restaurant on any given day. We're never guaranteed customers. In fact, there are really no guarantees at all in this field of work. Because of that fact, most banks, if not all, won't lend money, especially to entrepreneurs in our business. Statistics show that 9 out of 10 restaurants will fail in their first year. Fact.

Now, I'm not just talking about not having customers, there are a lot of ways to sink a ship. What if the people do come but the restaurant has internal problems like employee theft, equipment failing, leaky roofs, plumbing issues, electrical problems *or an excess of operating funding going towards the replacement of all those stolen sugar packets.* At any rate, it's like owning a house. In a house, the fridge breaks—get a five hundred dollar fridge. Have you ever had to buy a new compressor for a walk-in cooler? What if the walk-in cooler compressor breaks down and so does the air conditioner unit? I hope you have a lot of capital to fix these problems.

Unlike in my home, I will go without until I can afford to repair or replace the broken item. But in the restaurant business I'm offering convenience to my customers and those conveniences are air conditioning, comfortable chairs, and heat, just to name a few. I also have ordinances with the health department that I need to follow. Keeping my refrigerators at

38 degrees is mandatory. The health department isn't going to walk into my house and site me for not having a working freezer. But in Ambition that freezer better be working when the health department walks in.

I never really understood all the financial aspects of this business while I worked for other employers. Unlike like all the corporations I've worked for, I thought restaurant owners had expense accounts for all the miscellaneous problems that occurred. How did that new floor get paid for? Who paid to replace all the broken glassware we broke because we were careless? Or the silverware we threw away from not taking it off the plates as we dumped off the remaining food-who paid for that? Painting the outside of the building, was that free? I took for granted all those free sandwiches I ate that I was offered as a shift meal. I never put together that the owner paid for those foods, fixes and refurbishings. Or the holiday bonus checks I received. I never really thought where that money came from. I just said thank you. *At least now I hope I did.*

My friend George's usual saying is, "Who doesn't have an extra five thousand dollars lying around?" Then he'll say, "There's no problem too big that throwing buckets of money at can't fix."

Of course the question is what and where are these buckets of money?

It's one thing if you have a leak in the ceiling at your home. Put out a drip pot and save up until you have enough to fix it. But when that same scenario happens in a public restaurant it's a whole different story. Something like that can chase people away forever. Would you go back to a restaurant if the roof was leaking and the drops of water were hitting your shoes? The miracle here at Ambition is that we're ready and we're quick on our feet.

It was raining heavily and the gutter pipe was backed up. So where did the water go? It went into the restaurant. Not all at once, thank goodness, but drip by drip, hitting the floor and splashing a couple sitting at table #9. Although they somehow didn't notice we did. Thinking quickly, we spilled a small glass of water on the floor by them. "Ooops, we're sorry. Here's a towel to dry off your shoes." They never knew it. We unclogged the drainpipe, stopped the leak and had happy dry customers. That was an easy fix. We don't like fooling guests like that but something's are better left unsaid, until now…sorry.

Now here we go again. The same gutter is clogged *again*. But this time it's Mother's Day Weekend and Parents Weekend at Union College. Because of Mother's Day Weekend, we are closing early at 3 p.m.

It was a beautiful sunny day when suddenly this dark cloud roared in over Schenectady at 2 p.m. and dumped four inches of water in one hour.

I noticed it first. The tell tale sign is the leak in the kitchen. (I have angels around me that protect me or I like to believe they do by offering me signs of "here comes trouble" but if you're quick enough you can stop it.) The leak from the clogged gutter started in the kitchen. Instantly, I knew to get outside, and onto the roof in the pouring rain to unclog the gutter.

But the restaurant was having a surge of customers who are coming in out of the rain—so many customers came in that we ran out of chairs as guests were bringing in the chairs from the patio. By 2:15 we're packed.

I finally got outside, up on the roof and unclogged the gutter. *Two minutes too late.*

I came back in, soaking wet, when Stacy said to me, "Marc, there's a leak out here!"

"Just put a pot under it," I said, getting ready again in the kitchen. "I can't do else anything right now!"

"Marc, you need more than a pot!"

There was a three-foot wide wall of water cascading from the ceiling into the restaurant.

Thanks to my good fortune, the waterfall was in the back where nobody sat but the water quickly covered the floor. The wait staff slopped back and forth through it to serve. *How lovely, our own personal Zen garden!*

By good grace alone, our guests didn't mind the water. *This kinda thing happens everyday.* They were rather empathetic throughout the ordeal. They were hungry and wanted something to eat. I guess they looked at it like entertainment in the meantime. *Kinda like dinner and a movie.*

The waterfall eventually did slow to a trickle. And although it was manageable to contain, what was the difference at this point? Water was covering the floor in a twenty-foot area. The wait staff shoes were soaked. I could go describing the scene as though it were nightmarish, but it was one of my happiest memories at Ambition. All the guests that day left happy.

I stayed late that day *(surprise)* to continue cleaning, and as I mopped the floors, I found a white feather that was dry right where this whole fiasco happened. I took a moment, looked up with a tear in my eye and gave thanks, because this situation could have gone so wrong. *There are days I feel truly blessed and this was one of them.*

It's hard work to run a successful restaurant. We have so many elements working against us. Customers steal, employees steal, owners steal, vendors steal. It's truly an amazing field of work. I know theft happens everywhere. Supermarkets, malls, banks, at the office using the fax machine for personal use, *some days it feels like everyone does, but in my heart I know better.* "I deserve it" is the motto of the thief. But do you really deserve it? You're hired to do a job. You're paid to do a job. So why do you feel you deserve more than just that? Is it because you work hard? A lot of people work hard. You stay overtime, a lot of people stay overtime. You're a team player. A lot of people are team players. Why do you deserve it? Why do you feel it's your right to use or take something that someone else bought?

Business owners like me believe that we have the best employees. Even though I'd like to believe they would never steal from me, it happens. One employee used to steal liquor. This person would drink four shots of anything, then a beer or two, then go throw it up in the bathroom because too much was consumed too fast. *(That sounds like great fun!)* I inventoried the bar and realized I was out of four top-shelf liquors. (If you're not in the business, top shelf is as it states, top of the line: your Grey Goose, Godiva, Absolut, Johnny Walker, etc.) Four of these were empty; you do the math.

Another employee would steal the wait staff's tips off the tables. *This builds employee moral!* Or better yet, the bartender would take the tips from the servers as he would cash out their guest checks. Forty dollars cash was left behind on a thirty-three dollar guest check. But the server only saw three dollars of it. That puts me in an awkward position as I now have to approach this bartender and ask where the rest of the money went. *And now I have to fire him. Lucky me.*

One employee even furnished their apartment with money from Ambition's loyal customer funding. Of course you could give them the benefit of the doubt but I have to say that this particular person didn't work for the money, just took it. Every theft analyst will tell you if your employees are living outside their means (what they earn for a salary is less then how they're living.) If so, then there is usually theft involved. Does your employee who was hard for money a few months ago now seem to have everything they want? (Laptop, Blackberry, iPod, to name a few things.) I would like to think my employees earn an honorable living at Ambition on their salaries but it's certainly not enough to purchase high-end gadgets like these new cell phones, Blackberries, iPod's, lap-top's, digital cable with HBO, Showtime, and every pay program available. When a few other high end items were added to this employees list, I realized I really need to keep a watch on the cash register and the bank bag. I've learned to match up the duplicate guest checks with the originals to make sure they match in everyway. I also review the register's printed receipt; to make sure that total matches with the guest checks. *Some employees were very clever.*

Although I was a day late and a few dollars short, I did fix the problem. This problem only cost about ten thousand dollars. It's only money; you can't take it with you. Talk about employee benefits, this takes it to a whole different level. After I fired this employee, they went on to collect their unemployment benefits. Now, contest this employee's grievance to New York State that this person stole cash and shouldn't be eligible for unemployment benefits. I lost the claim and add insult to injury, not only was the money stolen, but also now my unemployment insurance is going up. *Thanks for everything!*

One employee worked for me a little over two years. It stings because I grew to trust this person after so much time. I relied on him; (I like how the word "lied" is in relied) I'd leave and the restaurant ran smoothly... or so I thought.

I left. The restaurant operated and guess what? I'm missing cash.

Let's look. It had been counted at 6:30 p.m., signed by so and so, who said it was accurate, and now I'm walking to the bank to make a deposit–*cue the suspense music*–and it's exactly $50 short.

So I decided to call the security system and ask for a printout of all the entries and exits registered for that day. I came to find out that this employee, who *had* a key *and* his own security code, *entered* the building at one in the morning, (probably to finish his beer run for the night) and took the money when the restaurant was closed. *Yes, it was Mr. Stupid, in the kitchen with the lead pipe.* Donald Trump, let me use you quote, "You're fired!" And the unemployment insurance game continues. Prove to New York State that person stole cash. *I get to pay even higher unemployment insurance, yippee!*

Another employee stole $60 from the register but was stupid enough to ring it up as a pay-out. Oh, but it gets better. He did it at a time when the restaurant was closed, and the time and date were printed on the dual receipt that the register prints. Explain your way out of that one. He tried saying someone must have waltzed into the restaurant and entered a $60 pay-out.

Thieves must be getting smart these days by trying to erase their paths. They're not just breaking open the register and taking the money. Now they're going to the extremes of taking the time to enter the dollar amount stolen from the register. *Brilliant! My accountant will be pleased to know he has less work to do.*

Still, another employee went through at least 90 cans of whipped cream. It's called a whippet. It's when the gas from a whipped cream can is sucked out, giving a six second rush. *It's a really fast act of stupidity while killing many brain cells. This is why the employee did so many cans of whipped cream, because he's stupid now!*

I would enter the walk-in cooler, reach for a whipped cream can, and the seal would be broken. Do you understand how annoying this is? (The can of whipped cream is ruined because all the air was released and it comes out like goo.) This went on for months, but, allegedly, nobody was doing it and nobody knew who it was either. I heard lots of excuses like, maybe it came in on the truck that way or maybe a delivery person did it, or maybe…. Needless to say I was cleaning out the upstairs of the restaurant in March of 2006 and in the extra insulation was a can of whipped cream with an expiration date of May, 2004. The length this person went through to get their little high was unreal. I hold this can of whipped cream at the Hoosier cabinet as a trophy to myself for financially surviving all these employees.

In the end, all these employees collectively stole well over $45,000. Thanks for everything! You were a great bunch of employees! Of course, nobody admits to anything. Restaurants are full of innocent people, just like jails.

We deal with a lot of vendors for food and merchandise. I try to be as honest and as faithful to my word and work as I can be. But this business is cutthroat. The profits are small. Everyone in the business is competing for the same dollar. Many resort to unethical practices to get their share. Enter my bread vendor. I've used the same bread vendor since our second year of business. For two years everything was perfect. Suddenly, the quality of the sourdough was on the decline. It was delivered with air bubbles throughout each loaf and I mean holes—right through one side of the loaf to the other. Now I ask, how can I make you a sandwich with bread like that? So I started to return the bread, asking for a refund. This worked for a little while.

After about three months of air pocket holes in the bread, the driver came in and said to me, "The owner told me to tell you that there are supposed to be holes in the bread." (Oh, really. Those big holes through the bread are supposed to be there. So then why doesn't anyone else offer such quality if they're supposed to be there?) Needless to say, the next week I dropped the company. The bread company later came back to me and confessed the problem. They excused the mistake attributing the problem to the new cook, kneading the dough. Because they came clean, I decided to stick with the company.

But then as they say, hindsight is 20-20. This same bread company then started sending me rye bread without any caraway seeds. I asked where the seeds were, and their response was the hospitals and schools were complaining about the seeds so they stopped using them. Sounded like a credible answer. Then, about two weeks later, the multi-grain bread started coming in as wheat. *Okay, hold it, what's going on here?* I called again and they confirmed that, yes, the multi-grain still has grains and the wheat doesn't. Then, why am I getting wheat when I ordered multi-grain?

"Oh, we're sorry. We made a mistake." This was Thursday. I called to order more bread again on Saturday. "We're out of business," said the receptionist.

What the hell happened? I call on Thursday, you take my order, I call again on Saturday and you're out of business? No notice, no nothing? (As I said, hindsight is 20-20.) The worst part about this situation was not having any bread when *Phantom of The Opera* rolled into town at Proctor's for a three-week run. My business turned upside-down and inside-out. What a huge economic boost the show was for Schenectady but what a headache for me. On top of all the extra business coming in from the show, I needed to look for a new bread company. We make *great* sandwiches, but we do need bread to do so. I had no bread and business was overwhelming. We had a new bread company in two days, but not before we made many trips to the local supermarket. Thanks, Neil Golub!

A new hired employee named Chrissy started working for Ambition. She's a soft-spoken young lady but she's dramatic. She's pissed over this and mad over that. Her pants got dirty or her shirt has a wrinkle or she broke a nail. You get the idea. One day, Chrissy came in and started to open up to get ready for lunch. Filling salt and pepper shakers, grabbing napkins, menus along with other things preparing for the lunch rush when she came around the corner and said, "Hey, guys, come here, come here." She went back around the corner but both Stacy and I ignored her. Chrissy came back around the corner and said again, "Hey, guys, seriously, come here, come here!" She went back around the corner again.

This time she was a little more convincing but both Stacy and I said, "Shut the hell up!"

The third time she returned, she really laid it on: "Guys, really, seriously come here, come here now!"

So Stacy went first, and she tore around the corner. My problem-radar went off; it's that beeping in my head as the time counts down to zero. So I put a little skip in my step when I started to hear water gushing as I turn the corner to go around the bar and into the dining room. The faucet head had blown off the faucet and--no lie--the water was shooting in the air like Old Faithful. It had to be ten or twelve feet. It was a geyser. We have fourteen foot ceilings in the dining room so it allowed room for this fountain. (I guess we have good water pressure here in Schenectady.) I went for the shut-off valve but it was behind a cabinet that's screwed to the wall. *I'm thinking to myself, who's the idiot who screwed screws into this wall? Oh, that was me.* Now here I was trying to unscrew these screws as the water was gushing out. Stacy grabbed one of our metal rectangular gelato pans and put it over the faucet. Although she was soaked, she kept the water in the sink.

Meanwhile, I was still trying to get the cabinet door off when Steve, from City Hall, came over.

"You guys have a little problem over here?" He laughed.

"No, Steve, this is how we wash dishes."

He laughed again and said, "Just put the faucet head back on again until you shut the water off."

Oh. Like why didn't I think of that? So Stacy took the gelato pan off the faucet and the water was back to shooting twelve feet into the air. We fumbled with the faucet head and, thankfully, capped it off.

A calm moment after the storm. Everything is silent. I look at Stacy who is dripping wet and I start laughing! She too eyes me up and down to assess the damages and together we look like two drowned cats. We now look over at the very dry Chrissy who was too afraid to get wet and I said, "The next time something like that happens, make sure you actually articulate that there is a problem. Don't just say, *come here, come here.*"

That whole water fountain trick was a nine hundred dollar loss since we had to repurchase all the prepackaged nostalgic candies that the water ruined. And, yeah, my insurance deductible is one thousand dollars. *Did I ever say how much I love paying for insurance?*

Water problems are the biggest problems at Ambition. If it's not a clogged bathroom then it's the roof leaking. If it's not a roof leak, it's a failing faucet. If not that then the bar sinks are clogged.

Call Al the plumber. Another $65 every time he picks up the phone for us. Contractors bill it under service calls. I wonder if I can start charging service calls for take-out orders. Yes, your Ambition sandwich will be $73. We added a service call charge! See you in 10 minutes. *Bring your mortgage.*

Welcome to the Northeast, where winters can be hell. Twenty-five degrees below zero does wonders on water pipes. A good freeze and a broken pipe and another grand down the drain. *It's funny how the drains never seem to get clogged when I flush all that money down.*

We did enjoy the time when the dishwasher broke; we hand washed the dishes all day long. That made the employees happy to come to work. It took four days for this little plastic part to come in which cost $36. Labor was added and my total bill was $436. That's when I realized that I was in the wrong profession. *Do all contractor's graduate from the same college of Screwum Cheetum and How?*

Then there's the grease trap. Anyone who owns a restaurant, manages, or gets paid to clean these beasts out knows how much fun they are and how delightful they smell. There's nothing quite like grease and decomposing food boiling and bubbling in this square metal trap. Just as you open that lid the smell hits you and your face falls off! Awesome! Can I offer you a cup of grease trap to go? Yet, another bill for removing the waste from the grease trap.

What do you do when the espresso machine doesn't shut off after its eighteen-second brew? "Uh, could I have another cup really fast, please?" Espresso was pouring out of the machine and we were pushing the stop button, and it just wasn't stopping. "What the hell is going on here?" It finally agreed with us and shut off. Thank goodness I'm paying for that maintenance contract at least when it breaks down, for some reason I feel like I'm getting my moneys worth.

How about when you're brewing a shot of espresso and the handle blows off the espresso machine? *Always a crowd pleaser*. Extremely hot water mixed with thousands of finely ground espresso beans all over you, the counter, the machine and the floor. *Pass the handy wipes.*

Our dual coffee brewer went on the fritz one day. The water started pouring out of the bottom of the machine. I guess the reservoir inside the brewer that holds the water sprang a leak. This happened during the noon rush. Water went everywhere. We had cups, mops and buckets trying to collect all the water. Unsuccessfully, I might add. And people are piling in for lunch. *Not a bad time at all!*

I turned a valve, which I believed to be the water shut-off, but the water still kept coming. So Stacy and I were standing in a puddle of water when I grabbed the metal bowl to dump the water that was collected. Doing so, it hit the bottom of the brewer where the electric cord is. Let's see, water and electric, uhm Yeah, Zappo! I took a pretty good zap, right up my arms. At the same time, Stacy grabbed the coffee bean dispenser, which was metal and switched "on." She got it too. *Zing! Zing!* We looked at each other, laughing, but pissed. I ran upstairs and flipped the breaker. As I did that, Stacy finally switched off the correct water valve. The unit was finally still. I will say though, I had great hair for the rest of the day. *And guess what? I got to use my maintenance contract again!*

A fun day was when the electric company visited us in the middle of lunch and wanted payment or they're going to shut the electric off right in the middle of lunch business. So I just whistle, usually some nursery rhyme because I act that old at these times of not paying my bills on time. Now I pretend this person in the jump suit with a big tool and hardhat isn't standing there. I pretend that the customers don't see him either. I write the check, and my day goes on. How old am I now? And I still don't have this whole bill-paying thing down yet. I would be a liar if I wrote that a day like this only happened once. Or better yet, would you believe me if I told you it only happened once? *I hear the "Jeopardy" theme song playing while you ponder that question.*

Our cash register shocked us one day as we closed the drawer. The next day it happened again, and again and again. Soon, everyone was getting shocked from the register as they closed the drawer. Then about a week later, I got it too. Zap! What the hell? So about another week went by and we were still being shocked from this register, but now the surge was getting stronger and really started to hurt. We started troubleshooting. What could possibly be doing this? The extension cord, or was it the register itself? There seemed to be many possibilities. We fixed one thing after another, but the shock was still there. So I called the electrician and told him to fix it. He did, or so we thought, until the shock was back the next day. And another $200 was safely spent and out the window.

I called the electrician again, ($60 dollar service fee) and told him to fix it again. (Are all these contractors in cahoots with each other?) Finally, we discovered the shocking truth— the outlet that the register was plugged into had a short. That whole scenario cost a total of $500. *But, it's only money; you can't take it with you.*

So what do you do when a squirrel runs in the restaurant? *My* answer was to scream like a little white girl. *That didn't quite fix the problem*, so we grabbed a sheet of plywood from outside and sort of cornered the squirrel, forcing it back to the door. My job was to open the door so the squirrel could run out. Nobody told me the squirrel was going to jump up into the booth I was in. Of course, I thought this squirrel was going to spin around, turn into *Cujo* and kill me. After many more screams on my part, we did finally get the squirrel out of the restaurant. Ambition 1, Squirrel 0. Although I never scheduled for a rematch, it happened again. A squirrel got into the restaurant. It came out when the restaurant closed and sat in the plants that are in the front window, for people to see as they walked by. People took pictures of this squirrel, "It was so cute," they said. And I received a picture in the mail of this squirrel. *Some people really need to get a hobby!*

Of course, a restaurant cannot have a squirrel running loose so we called Ace Pest Control and they brought over a Have-A-Heart trap and they caught the squirrel. Two hundred and fifty dollars later the Problem was solved. Or so I thought. A person thought I liked having this squirrel in the restaurant so they called the Health Department and told them I have a squirrel *living* in the restaurant. The Health Department showed up, investigated the situation, saw the bill from Ace Pest Control and left. Laughing with me the Health Department said, "It happens, squirrels have been here longer then us. We just need to follow through with the complaint." *Ambition 2, Squirrels 0.*

People who want to own restaurants do not understand that once the restaurant opens, they're there for twenty-four hours a day, seven days a week. (Sometimes I think I should have signed a prenup.) Who else is going to take care of the walk-in cooler when it breaks down at 1a.m.? Who else is going to care if the ceiling is leaking over night? Who else is going to care if, on a Sunday (the only day the restaurant is closed and you have plans), a pipe bursts. Welcome to ownership of a restaurant, it's all yours! Once again, unlike homeownership, the equipment is used so much more then in a home that these problems happen much more frequently.

We made *gelato* on Monday and put it in the *gelato* case (a freezer unit) for display. It looked beautiful! When I arrived on Tuesday morning we had soup. It looked like the Wicked Witch from *The Wizard of Oz*, after Dorothy melted her with water.

First thing, the money I just lost from the melted product that sat warm in the case over night. Second, the labor I just lost that this employee was paid to make the gelato. Third, the added expense for a new compressor is $700. Fourth, how many days was the *gelato* case down that I received no return on my money but yet I was still paying maintenance fees, product fees, labor, (how do I expect to pay the bill for those cute little plastic cups and spoons I bought if no money is coming in.) My employees didn't care that the unit broke down; they just want their paycheck on Friday, period! And it's my responsibility to pay the employees on Friday. *You know what, I can't pay you today because the gelato case broke down and no money came in so you'll have to wait to get paid when it's fixed.* Oh, that will be the day. Reach deep down in those pockets of mine! Fifth, this is when the director yelled, "Take, Two!" The whole process starts again. The *gelato* case is fixed and we start all over. The labor...the product..., but this time I started in the negative because I now have to make up all that money that was lost. *Better get to scooping that gelato!*

A real kick in the pants is when people see how busy we are and just assume I'm rolling in money. I don't have one problem and life is just wonderful! The money is rolling in and I'm happy, happy, happy! So they ask me for a donation. They say, "You're busy today! Would you mind donating to our cause? We accept donations for amounts over $100." *Sure! I just lost $2,000 because my gelato case broke down, but what's another hundred dollars!*

Equipment in a restaurant operates twenty-four hours a day and seven days a week. Would you like to pay my electric bill? This is similar to operating four laundry driers in your house. Now do it twenty-four hours a day. Imagine your bill. Yeah, your eyes will fall out of your head.

This equipment is made to operate this way. The catch is when they break just imagining the cost of fixing the equipment. I have a walk-in cooler, a reach-in cooler, two soda coolers, *gelato* case, candy case, two air conditioners, a freezer, and a *gelato* machine to make the *gelato*. I've had to replace the compressors on all of these machines once so far. Just keep reaching down in those pockets. *Maybe I should have kept my parachute pants from the 80's and shoved all my money in the many pockets.*

CHAPTER 13

My Greatest Mistakes

I guess I have a talent for being able to know what food is going to taste like without trying it. I know which ingredients go well together and how they can complement each other to make a great sandwich or dinner. Friends, Rich and Chari, tell me, "You have calibrated fingers." By this they mean that I can feel something and know it's the right amount—a tablespoon of this, a cup of that, a pound of flour—all without using measuring cups.

So here's where my calibrated fingers came to my rescue and the story behind the bread pudding.

I needed to make a bread pudding for an evening's function. I knew *what* went in bread pudding, but I didn't know how much. I started thinking, and grabbed the usual ingredients, heavy cream, eggs, cinnamon, bread, sugar. I mixed it up and didn't think it was sweet enough. So I grabbed mini chocolate chips and sprinkled them on top with a little more cinnamon, baked it for what I thought was a good amount of time and served it. That was the start of the phenomenon of the bread pudding. No recipe, just guessing, but the customers took right to it and have said it was the best they ever had. Some of those customers claim to be bread pudding experts and have bread pudding everywhere they go. "Yours is the best."

A mother of a Union College student told me her son was working as a chef in NYC and asked if she could have the recipe so he could use it at the restaurant he worked in.

Schenectady has a public access TV station and I was asked to make a bread pudding on that show. This list of compliments goes on and on and on, and I'm as humble as I can be. It was sheer luck as I look at it but at the same time, it was meant to be. I've sold countless pans of bread pudding over the years and have *never* given out the recipe *until now*.

I've always guarded these recipes in fear thinking someone would steal and copy them. But in life, I'm learning the more you give and the more you share, the more you'll receive. These recipes below are my crown jewels of Ambition and I offer them to you to enjoy and to share.

BREAD PUDDING

(This is for a 9 x 14 inch pan.) Spray the pan with non-stick spray. Preheat oven 375°

1½ quarts of heavy cream

6 eggs

2 tablespoons of cinnamon

1¼ cup of sugar

1 pound of bread (cubed, sourdough, white, wheat, multi grain, potato, anything but rye) I use freshly baked bread at Ambition. This bread is much denser then the spongy processed type from those big bread manufacturing companies. So your ratio may be off if you use those breads. Which will work, but you'll need to adjust accordingly.

¾ cup mini chocolate chips

Mix the eggs, cream, cinnamon and sugar together, leaving behind one tablespoon of cinnamon and the chocolate chips. Add the bread. The bread should be submerged in the mixture. The mixture should be loose, but not too liquidy. Put the mixture in the greased pan. Sprinkle the last tablespoon of cinnamon over the top and add the mini chocolate chips. Bake it in the oven for 50 minutes. The top should be golden brown and bubbling around the sides. Let it sit for about a half hour to set up. Then eat, eat, eat! It's best served when warm or warmed in the microwave oven. Serve with whipped cream and caramel syrup. Portion size depends on you and on how many people you want the pan to feed. The pan size will feed up to 20 people. Holds well, covered in the refrigerator for a week. I've never frozen this product so I don't know how it will react.

BALSAMIC VINAIGRETTE

I have a sweet tooth, so I use sugar in the vinaigrette. People always ask me, "What's in the dressing, how do you make it? I love it! You should bottle the dressing and sell it."

Quarter green pepper
Quarter red onion
Quarter red pepper
½ T white pepper
½ T garlic powder
1 T sugar
1 T Dijon
1 T dried basil
2 cups balsamic
2 cups oil

In a blender, add all ingredients except vinegar and oil and blend well. Add the balsamic vinegar, blend again, and then slowly add the oil. Perfect.

I've also added raspberry or orange flavoring to this dressing and it only compliments it. Try it with different flavors and see how it works for you.

My food sales representative came in and offered me a sample of black bean burgers. They were tasty. Now he wanted to sell me a case of black bean burgers, nicely packaged, bagged, but frozen. I said, "You know I don't buy frozen foods. But sell me dried beans and I'll make my own burgers." This really was a challenge to myself because I wanted to make a better black bean burger then what I was presented by my sales rep. So with my ego pushed aside, that's how these came about:

BLACK BEAN BURGER

1-12 oz bag dried black beans
1 green pepper
1 red pepper
1 red onion
2 T cumin
2 cups plain bread crumbs
3 eggs
Salt /pepper (to taste)

Soak the black beans overnight in a container. In a tail pot, bring the soaked beans to boil and cook until soft, about one hour. In the food processor add both peppers and onion and blend. Place in a separate bowl. Blend all the black beans in food processor and puree. Add the pureed beans to the vegetables. Add the eggs, cumin, salt/pepper to taste and stir in the breadcrumbs. Portion out the burgers (our portion is five ounces). Though we don't, you can feel comfortable freezing these. When ready to eat, heat on a flat pan, searing both sides just to heat the product. We use a sun-dried tomato ciabatta with pepper jack cheese, homemade salsa, with lettuce and tomato to finish the sandwich.

Another instant smash are the crab cakes. Yes, we use real crabmeat in our crab cakes. But it's a 50/50 blend of real mixed with imitation to keep the product cost reasonable. I often hear guests tell me how wonderful these crab cakes are because most other restaurants often use too much bread crumbs. And we don't fry them either. We heat them on our flat-top or in a sauté pan. Guests like it as a healthy option.

CRAB CAKES

1 lb. Phillip's canned crabmeat
1 lb. imitation crab
3 eggs
1 1/2 cups mayo
2 T Old Bay Seasoning
2 cups plain breadcrumbs

In a bowl, shred the imitation crab so it's flaky then mix both crabmeats together. Add the eggs, mayo and Old Bay seasoning and stir. Finish by stirring in the breadcrumbs. We weigh out the crab cakes in 5-ounce portions and pan sear them on both sides until golden brown. We make our own remoulade, and serve the crab cake with pita points and a side salad.

There've been many great recipes we've used at Ambition. Some of my greatest ideas have been from traveling around to other restaurants whether on vacation or just an evening out, something that I liked and then put my own twist on it. I usually change the ingredients just to keep it original. I will go out for dinner and make a sandwich out of the entrée I had. I also meditate and through that came some great ideas. I accept any help. A good friend told me, originality is the ability to conceal your sources. So, to all you great chefs out there, thank you. And if I've inspired some great chefs, well then you're welcome. Pay it forward.

My Dream Came True

We've served tens of thousands of happy and appreciative customers who have gone unnoticed throughout this book. Like Roberta Steiner who gave me a decorative light switch cover for the lady's bathroom. Generous, kind, warm-hearted, and grateful people who are thankful Ambition is here in Schenectady. Families whose siblings live in other cities tell us, every time we come home, we come here. What a wonderful affiliation to be thought of when thinking of home. I am truly blessed and I wish I can say thank you to all of those customers who've made my journey successful. Well, I guess I can. *I thank you very sweetly for visiting us daily, monthly or weekly!*

It has taken a few years to write this book and in that time a lot of people have come to me and said what a great job we're doing here or how great the sandwiches are or just, "We're happy you're here." It's a beautiful thing to hear. I've also received letters from customers saying what a great time they had at Ambition or that the bread pudding you cooked for me was the hit of the party. One woman in particular liked our mugs at the restaurant.

We have a pottery store named Two Spruce Pottery on Jay Street that makes our coffee mugs. Nancy the owner does a great job making them colorful. That's what I always say to her: "make them wild and colorful."

But this one woman in particular liked her mug *so* much; I gave the mug to her. The letter she sent me thanking me was so sincere. She wrote she had come out to lunch with a friend to discuss her mother's health issues. It continued on how some tears were shed, some laughter but through the conversations was "this mug" she liked so very much. As she wrote, "It fit perfectly in my hand. It has cats on it and I'm a cat lover." She finished her note with she will always use her mug and think of Ambition and our generosity.

I touched someone's life and made her happy. That's a great feeling. How often do we really touch other people's lives? Do we really care to? I do.

I put my heart and soul into Ambition and through it all, through the bills, the taxes, the electricity, breaking pipes, leaking ceilings, clogged toilets, theft, the crazy customers, family deaths, through it all, I love this business. I wouldn't change a thing if I could. I wouldn't change any of the heartache because it makes the success that much sweeter.

I've read of people writing about success and failure and saying not to quit just hold on through one more day. There were many days when I said, "That's it! That's enough. Just sell the place!" But then I think about all the happiness owning Ambition has brought me. I wake up most days happy to go to work. *Happy to be at work, even if it is for twelve hours.* The joy I bring to my life and to other people's lives. Sometimes just saying, "I like your shoes," can make a person's day—*even if they're red.* Something as small as that can touch people on their worst day and make them smile. That's what it's all about.

A female customer of mine was getting married. She confided that she thought she was too heavy. The woman was a size 8 at best. Her husband-to-be also made the mistake of agreeing with her. This really allowed her insecurities to take off. I looked at her and said, "You're a beautiful woman. I wish you could see yourself through my eyes." She just started to cry. I immediately felt awful for what I thought was hurting her feelings but didn't know what to do.

Then she said to me through tears, "That was the nicest thing anyone has said to me in a long time." What a wonderful feeling that is, again, to make someone happy.

Tommy Tune was in the restaurant while he was touring with his show, *Dr. Doolittle*, at Proctor's. Now, most people know who Tommy Tune is by his height alone but if you don't, he's a well established Broadway actor/director. Winning 9 Tony's on Broadway through his career. Tommy was in all that week and was just looking around and said to me, "You love what you do and it shows." Tommy made me so proud that day. What a great feeling that was. To me, that's what owning a restaurant is about, connecting with people, directly or indirectly.

Think about *Cheers* and its characters Sam, Norm, Rebecca, Carla, Cliff or how about *Alice* at Mel's Diner with Flo and Vera. The sitcoms *Friends* or *Seinfeld*, (I'm sure the *Soup Nazi* wasn't always angry, but how did he become angry? That would have been a funny episode.) *Happy Days*, how happy were we to be there with Al, the Fonz, the Cunninghams and the whole gang. Think about any restaurant that you have ever been to and enjoyed so much that you went to work and told your colleagues about it. "Oh, my God, did you see all the pictures? I had the best sandwich. It was so good, and they have bread pudding that's to die for. It's just the cutest little place. Oh, you've been there, too?" It's called "buzz", and Ambition has it. *I don't know who gave it to her but I'm truly thankful she has it.* There's something magical about restaurants that can create this atmosphere of nostalgia and sexiness. Think about your favorite restaurant (hopefully it's Ambition) and ask yourself why you like it so much. There are probably many more reasons besides the fact that they make good turkey sandwiches. If Ambition is your favorite, then the answer is probably the employees, the atmosphere, my personality, (take Madonna, Cyndi Lauper and Dolly Parton and put them all together and that's me, minus the boobs), it's the menu, the prices, the offerings, the coffee club cards (that are hand designed by my niece Jessica), maybe it's our four foot disco ball, maybe because you come for Blackboots. Many people do.

People talk about *Playboy*'s playmates and men in uniforms because they're sexy. There's a certain buzz they create. If a restaurant can create that feeling it's sure to have a great business life. Whenever we talk about our lives, it's usually when food is around. Now food can be as simple as a cup of coffee. But when we really get down to the heart and soul of life and we laugh and cry, look around and I bet there will be some sort of food nearby. Food is comfort. And in this day and age we all could use some comfort.

So to everyone who has entered my life since I opened on April 10, 2000, I thank you from the bottom of my heart for coming on this journey with me. I thank you for sharing your lives with me. I've met some very colorful people along this journey. And I still wouldn't change any of it. *Because I know now they were there for me, for my journey and for this book.* I hope you've enjoyed reading this as much as I've enjoyed owning and operating Ambition. True happiness is being able to live your dreams. I can only hope this book finds the people it's supposed to and inspires them to live fuller, richer lives.

Allow yourself to imagine, dream, and create a better place. You deserve it. Now go out there and get it. And don't ever let anyone stand in the way of your dreams. Any person who ever made anything out of their life is because they dreamed it first.

And yes, the coffee at Ambition is and always will be... fresh! And it will be waiting there, *for you.*

Peace.

Fondly yours,
Marc
Not so crabby once you get to know me.

Closing Time

It's 5:14 p.m. and finally all the guests have left. It's just the crew and me. All of us are busy doing our own thing as quickly as possible. Even though Ambition is beautiful, we all need to get home once in a while. I grab the plastic and wrap any exposed food in my reach-in cooler: chicken breasts, crab cakes, black bean burgers and pickles. Next, I turn off the flat-top. Letting that cool, I sweep the floor and take the garbage out. I wipe down all my stainless steel doors and bleach my cutting boards. By this time the flat-top is cool enough to clean, so I grab my stone and start scrubbing, finding the beautiful shine that was there this morning. Wipe my flat-top down, and I shut off my hood fans. I grab the broom again and sweep the restaurant, under each booth, table, chairs and bar stools… all the way through to the lounge. *My favorite job*, I clean the bathrooms and then grab the mop and mop bucket. I fill it with hot water, lemon-scented Pine-Sol and start mopping. My kitchen is now clean and so are all the floors. After everything is shining and dry, I grab the croissants and lay them out to proof for the next day. I do my final inventory walk-through and place any produce order, bread order or make a list of anything that I may need for the next day.

My staff is counting the register, restocking inventory: cups, lids, straws, napkins, salt and pepper shakers (if they made it through the day). They're dumping the extra coffee and milks that weren't used, cleaning the espresso machine, putting the lemons and the iced tea in the cooler. They wipe down all the tables, the bar area, and clean the last of the dishes. I give a little throw back to my employees with a shift drink at the end of the day while we clean. I shut off the lights, first in the lounge, then the track lighting over the coffee station and the bar lights. I grab a seat at the bar with the staff. We sit for a few minutes, unwind, talking about the day, everything that was said, the things that went wrong, or the things that went right (e.g. the annoying person at table #6 or the really hot dude who came in for take-out.) Usually we laugh at the day. We know we're done when we say, "I'm ready to go home," and we get up and walk towards the door.

I press the away button on the security pad and the countdown beeping begins. We all walk single file to the door, holding the door open because it can only close once or it sets the alarm off. (Not like that hasn't been done several times already, causing the police to swing by. Oops!) I turn off the remaining lights, and, as I close the door I always say, "Thank you" to Ambition, put the key in the lock, and turn it again full circle. The lock clicks, the door locks and my day is done.